D1451914

The Knowledge Value Chain® Handbook

Version 4.0

Timothy W. Powell

THE knowledgeagency®

New York, New York, USA

AN EYES AND EARS BOOK
PUBLISHED BY THE KNOWLEDGE AGENCY® (TKA), A DIVISION OF TW POWELL CO.

The Knowledge Agency
548 West 28th Street
New York, NY 10001
USA

Version 4.0

ISBN: 978-0-9798414-2-2

Slide designs by John Fantini and Tim Powell

Book design by John Fantini

Some contents published previously as *The Knowledge Value Chain® Workbook*
US Copyright TXu1-359-935

Author's web site: *The Knowledge Agency* www.KnowledgeAgency.com

Author's blog: *Competing in the Knowledge Economy* www.KnowledgeValueChain.com

For the sources of the greatest value in my life:

Ellen, Mike, and Dave

Also by Tim Powell:

Analyzing Your Competition

The High-Tech Marketing Machine

CONTENTS

The Knowledge Value Chain® Handbook—Introduction

Competing in the knowledge economy

Knowledge is a fundamental resource of our economic lives. If you were going to enter the business of, say, manufacturing airplanes, you would want to hire people with substantial applied expertise in the sciences of metallurgy, electronics, and even polymers—all the basic building blocks of your product.

Most of us work and compete in what is widely acknowledged to be a knowledge-based economy. But we do not have a science of knowledge—because there isn't one yet. Philosophy has a branch called *epistemology* that discusses the origins and characteristics of human knowledge—but that doesn't qualify as a science in the sense that technologies and management practices can be consistently derived from its principles.

Even the basic economics of knowledge are open to study and debate. Classical economists like Adam Smith generally did not regard knowledge as a key economic component. The "factors of production" were land, labor, and capital—with knowledge and information barely mentioned as being essential to production.

The fourth factor

Modern economists have begun to recognize knowledge as the "fourth factor" of production, and have gathered some insights into how it behaves. Fritz Machlup of Princeton University was one of the first to measure the knowledge macro-economy in 1962. By 1968, Peter Drucker described the knowledge worker's central role in creating productivity and competitiveness. Kenneth Arrow (and subsequent financial economists) worked on knowledge-related issues such as asymmetries of information in financial markets.

But these findings, however interesting, have limited applicability in a typical business setting. This is partly because the measurement of knowledge as an economic asset is at best inexact. Current financial accounting addresses knowledge only indirectly—as intellectual property assets and/or good will.

Organizational leaders sense that knowledge is important as a strategic resource, yet we don't know how to measure or manage it—or how to discuss it at more than a basic level.

Why is this a problem?

As Big Data becomes more common practice in many industries, people are concerned about data overload and about making sure the right information gets analyzed. These problems—common to nearly all organizations, large and small—are only getting worse, and soon will be of urgent concern at the highest levels of leadership.

Big Data, as promising as it is, can fail to the extent that it neglects the key first step in the Plan-Produce-Present sequence. By collecting data without prior regard to the need for hypothesis testing or any other *value-down* structure, it can create a *data-up* mentality that challenges the limits of the analytic and sense-making resources of the enterprise.

Big Data tempts us to look through the wrong end of the telescope. By looking up from the data end, things can seem unnecessarily confusing—even overwhelming. Viewing things value-down helps avoid most data overload problems.

The KVC framework is easy to understand and apply because it builds on a simple insight: in a complex organization, the people who produce information (producers) are fundamentally different from the people who use it to create results and value (users). This creates a *knowledge-value gap* between producers and users that is often vast—some call it a "gulf"—and includes many professional and cultural barriers.

In short, information people don't typically understand the language of business, and business people don't typically understand the language of information. The connection between the two halves—*the knowledge value chain*—is broken.

The net result is that information resources and the people who manage them fail to have the impact they could have, and fail to optimize their return on investment. Instead of being part of the organizational solution, information becomes part of the problem as people scurry to absorb and make sense of it.

Understanding the knowledge value chain from both producer and user perspectives is a first step toward bridging this fundamental barrier.

The knowledge factory

I've done a lot of research in my career—starting with work in a biomedical engineering lab and moving to focus groups and large-scale surveys and competitive analysis. Over time I realized that all research efforts contain the same essential steps. This insight became the foundation of the KVC model.

During the 1990s I managed research teams at a global research company (FIND/SVP, now part of ORC International) that employed about 300 people, most of whom worked in one block-long, high-ceilinged room (a former New York City clothing store). It was less like an office than a factory—but it was full of *knowledge workers* instead of factory workers. This was, essentially, a *knowledge factory.*

In business school courses on production processes and operations research, I had been trained to rigorously analyze factory work. I reasoned that, by extension, knowledge work could be analyzed in much the same ways.

A knowledge process model

I began drawing a diagram on the back of an envelope to explain to clients what stage our work was in, and what the next work steps would be. I pictured knowledge work as essentially a manufacturing process, with raw materials, work in process, and finished goods. This helped make the process more tangible and comprehensible to my colleagues and clients.

The back of the envelope sketch evolved and was published in its first form in an intelligence textbook (Gilad and Herring, *The Art and Science of Business Intelligence Analysis*) in 1996. Since then I've been able to travel the world telling people about my insight and how it might help them in their organization.

One rewarding result has been that when people hear about my work, they're often able to directly relate it to their own challenges or previous experiences. I have incorporated many of these client contributions into the work, a feedback process that has only enriched it (and me) over time.

The role of this book

This handbook is a user's manual to the *process* of organizational intelligence. In the ways that techniques such as Total Quality Management (TQM), Six Sigma, and Business Process Management are designed to increase the quality, efficiency, and effectiveness of manufacturing processes, the KVC is designed to do the same for knowledge-based processes.

This book does not address the *content* of intelligence. There are no sections on sources of data or techniques of analysis. I have addressed these in an earlier book, *Analyzing Your Competition*. But my focus here is purely on the intelligence process.

The KVC is one component in a systematic practitioner-focused study of knowledge and intelligence that I have undertaken. In my 2001 lecture series, *Knowledge: The Engine of Value* (presented as a SCIP MasterClass and elsewhere), the KVC made up only 15 (5.4%) of my 276 slides. And when I developed a graduate-level university course in 2005, *Enterprise Intelligence*, the KVC made up 38 (18.5%) of my 205 slides.

My goal is to publish some of these other findings soon. Because process is a key structural element and a lever for improvement, it makes an ideal starting point.

Broken intelligence

The ideas here were developed with two major trends as backdrop: (1) the repeated failures of intelligence in both business and civil affairs, and (2) the increasing use of return on investment (ROI) tests in the corporate world.

Significant intelligence failures in our time seem to come at regular, fairly short intervals. My new firm was just a toddler when the dot-com bubble of 2000-2001 caused the entire stock market to crash.

When I watched the twin towers of New York's World Trade Center burning on the morning of September 11, 2001, I wondered why—with so many people working in intelligence—we were not able to prevent it, and why we seemed so slow to react.

Leading up to the US invasion of Iraq in 2003, intelligence about presumed "weapons of mass destruction"—later found to be flawed—led to a long, costly war that could possibly have been avoided.

The mortgage bubble and crisis of 2008 revealed that—despite the legions of analysts watching every financial transaction—basic safeguards had been ignored. Few people saw this coming until it was too late to stop it.

Given all these unpleasant surprises, one would expect that professional foresight would have been highly valued and sought after. Yet people in the knowledge, intelligence, analysis, and forecasting disciplines seemed to find it increasingly difficult to prove their worth to their employers. During the great recession of 2008-2009, I saw the disciplines of competitive intelligence, knowledge management, and special libraries sputter and stall as executives cut back any resources that had such an (apparently) indirect connection to the top line.

I realized that what had at first seemed paradoxical—reductions in intelligence at the same time that intelligence seems so critical—was not such a paradox. I considered the possibility that the intelligence function simply hadn't been doing its job sufficiently. I began to see a consistent story of process failure—one that urgently needed to be remedied, and that *could* be remedied with diligent study and work.

I wanted to arm knowledge workers with the basic tools to understand the arguments of ROI and value that were, in many cases, being used against them. As a by-product, I reasoned that this would help them do their work to a higher standard of quality.

I finally concluded that the two trends listed at the top of this section (intelligence failure and a call for intelligence ROI) were actually two aspects of the same problem—a fundamentally broken intelligence process.

The process solution

Yogi Berra got it right when he said, "Prognostication is difficult—especially about the future." It is easy, after the fact, to see errors in intelligence. The hard part is to see them before they occur—and to correct them in time, or to prevent them entirely.

The solution to broken intelligence that I propose took me back to the key insight that designers of TQM and related manufacturing quality programs had in the 1970s—that quality is best built into a process, not tacked on at the end. This idea was making a huge impact when I was entering the workforce as a consultant.

Why wouldn't this insight apply equally well to intelligence and other "knowledge manufacturing" processes? I believe it does—and that's a core thesis of this book.

How the KVC works

The KVC sits at the intersection of how an organization produces value and how it processes information, or "thinks." A comprehensive KVC analysis is a snapshot of how information is deployed strategically—the functional analogue of a brain scan for an organization.

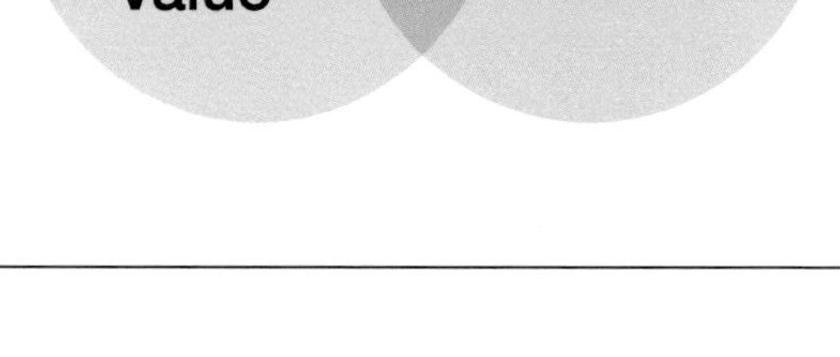

Your organization

How it produces value

How it 'thinks'

The KVC model proposes a close linkage between the *production* of knowledge and the *use* or application of that knowledge. It acknowledges, however, that in a complex, modern organization these two functions are most often separated by job function—with production being the responsibility of knowledge workers—analysts and researchers—and use being the responsibility of executives or decision-makers.

Each of the two halves is further divided into stages of processing (to fit our manufacturing analogy): Production, consisting of **Data**, **Information**, and **Knowledge**; and Use, consisting of **Decisions**, **Actions**, and **Value**. The linkage between the two halves—the bridge between knowledge production and use—is called **Intelligence**. Intelligence enables knowledge to be deployed as a strategic resource within the organization.

Clear distinctions are drawn between each *State* or stage of processing. While we try to maintain these distinctions clearly within this book, sometimes there is overlap—especially between "knowledge" and "intelligence."

The KVC model details the incremental effort and investment needed to get from one State to the next (*Transforms*, or Action Steps). At each State there are goals to be achieved (*value positives*) as well as pitfalls to be avoided (*value negatives*).

As with any manufacturing process, each State requires a level of completeness before moving to the next higher State. A *gate,* or test of readiness, is recommended.

Modes

In practice, the KVC model operates in three sequential modes: Planning, Production, and Presentation. In **Planning** a knowledge initiative, we step backward through the model from top to bottom. In other words, we decide what the Value payout of the effort is expected to be—the benefits or business results. This informs each lower level, until finally data needs can be defined and specified.

In the **Production** mode—the execution of the initiative—the reverse order is followed. We start with data acquisition, move into analysis, then communicate, and so on up the chain.

In the **Presentation** mode, things again move from the value-relevant sections down. In our *economy of attention*, when presenting research findings to a busy executive, always start with the "So Whats"—the most value-relevant findings—before moving down into the "Whats"—the detailed findings and methodology.

In practice the distinctions between the states may not be so clearly delineated. If you find, for example, that your analysis can't be completed without further data, you may need to cycle back for more data. As with most models, the KVC is an idealized, even aspirational, picture of how things actually work. But it gives us a framework and language for seeing how things do actually work—or fail to work.

Applications of the KVC framework

I first developed the KVC framework as a description of what I do for a living. Some people find knowledge work ethereal or mysterious, and this was intended to make it more transparent and concrete.

The KVC describes the DNA of fact-based decision-making. Once you understand its fundamental building blocks, you can apply it in situations with a wide range of scale and scope.

I originally used the KVC framework as a **Projects** level assessment, to help structure research projects my group was working on. Since then we've used it both on a smaller scale to assess individual knowledge **Products** (for example, reports), and on a larger scale to assess enterprise-level work **Processes** (for example, intra- and inter-departmental workflows).

Real-world applications of the KVC model have evolved over time, depending on the needs and situations of our clients.

Training. We have used the KVC in workshops and clinics to sensitize intelligence producers to the needs and perspectives of their clients. Once producers understand how users think about ROI, they are much better equipped to effectively address those users' needs.

Training for users is equally effective. For example, one of our clients in the pharmaceutical industry uses the model to illustrate to his board of directors how the research process works.

Diagnostics and workflow improvements. We have used the KVC to identify areas in a company's knowledge process that need strengthening—increased efficiency and/or effectiveness. This led to the step-by-step diagnostics that you'll see in the *KVC Scorecard.*

For example, in the case of another pharma company, we identified how internally developed information on rival products could be shared between R&D scientists and sales teams at various points in the development-production-sales cycles.

Research program design, planning, and management. We have applied the KVC as a key part of enterprise-level assessments of strategic intelligence readiness. In one case, we developed a roadmap of how a large health care corporation's strategic research needs would change as a result of wide-scale industry change brought on by health care reform.

In effect, we adapted the KVC model from a data-up diagnostic tool to a value-down prescriptive tool. We used it to develop a research strategy and roadmap that both increased our clients' effectiveness and reduced research redundancies.

This value-down approach makes the KVC especially useful to organizations deciding how to address and capitalize on "Big Data" analytics.

Career management. The human stories around the KVC are the most gratifying for me. I'll never tire of hearing from individual knowledge workers about how the KVC helped them do their job better, helped them explain to co-workers what they do, or helped them get hired because they had detailed knowledge of the process.

Who is the KVC's audience?

The KVC can help anyone who produces, manages, or uses intelligence in helping organizations achieve their goals. We've found that people in the following intelligence producer disciplines typically receive immediate benefits from the KVC:

- Business Strategy
- Corporate Intelligence
- Corporate Library
- Information Technology
- Knowledge Management
- Market Research
- Research and Development

Intelligence users, including C-suite executives, use the KVC to become better-informed, sophisticated buyers and users of intelligence. They tend to be interested in the tangible ROI benefits the KVC can yield. For example, for the health care client mentioned earlier, we restructured their corporate research functions to increase their strategic effectiveness while saving them about 20% of their research budget.

How to use this book

The *Handbook* started as annotated PowerPoint slides to structure and supplement our KVC workshops and clinics. These events were most often attended by intelligence producers, and much of the content reflects that perspective.

People wanted access to the slides if they weren't able to attend a KVC event. In 2008 we launched *The KVC Workbook* as a stand-alone publication.

For this edition we've renamed it *The KVC Handbook,* because we intend it to be used both as a training text and as an operating reference. It's really a "user's manual" for the KVC.

The text on each page explains and expands on—but does not replace—what is in the slide. You'll get the greatest benefit if you read each slide first to get the high notes and then read the accompanying text.

To show you how things play out in practice, we have paraphrased client quotes from our *Intelligence Points of Pain* research. We have also provided case examples from TKA consulting engagements.

Technical terms are typically in italics. When they are described or defined on the slide, they are in bold italics. Terms used frequently are defined in the Glossary in the Appendix.

We intend the *Handbook* and Clinic as more than just "knowledge." They are meant to help you solve your organization's problems. There is a section in the Appendix *(KVC Scorecard)* that presents a self-scoring diagnostic to help get you started.

We recommend you begin in the way we open many of our clinics and workshops—by writing a few words describing each of your 3-5 biggest intelligence or knowledge challenges. Have some colleagues do this too. You'll have the beginnings of a Points of Pain database that you can use to identify where in the chain your problems are and how to fix them.

A note on pronouns

We're not comfortable making everyone a "he," yet find it tiresome writing "he/she" and "his/her." Herein we're often discussing the hypothetical intelligence producer (the analyst) and the intelligence user (the client). Purely arbitrarily and expediently, we've made the former male, the latter female.

Updates

We post updates about the KVC on our web site www.KnowledgeValueChain.com. These include new applications of the KVC, listings of upcoming public appearances, KVC-related services, and additions and corrections.

We would benefit greatly from your input and feedback, especially if you've been using the KVC. This is how the model evolves.

The *KVC Handbook* is based on the slides to our intelligence clinic *The Knowledge Value Chain®: Raising the ROI of Intelligence.* The book was developed for use by participants during this clinic, and later was sold as a stand-alone hard copy book.

Except where noted, this is original content authored by Tim Powell, founder and president of research and consulting firm The Knowledge Agency® (TKA). The KVC model was developed by Powell in 1996, and various versions of this clinic have been given around the world since that time. This content was recently part of a graduate level university course on competitive intelligence, and is now its fourth major update.

TKA offers the KVC Clinic, as well as assessments based on the KVC framework. To stay informed on developments in the KVC, please see www.KnowledgeValueChain.com. Other TKA products and services are described at www.KnowledgeAgency.com.

We hope you'll benefit from what we present here, and that you'll tell others about your experience. Be aware, though, that the intellectual property contained here is owned by the TW Powell Co. d/b/a The Knowledge Agency®, and may not be copied, licensed, or resold without our written permission. Limited fair use quotes are permitted, but be sure to give us attribution if you do so.

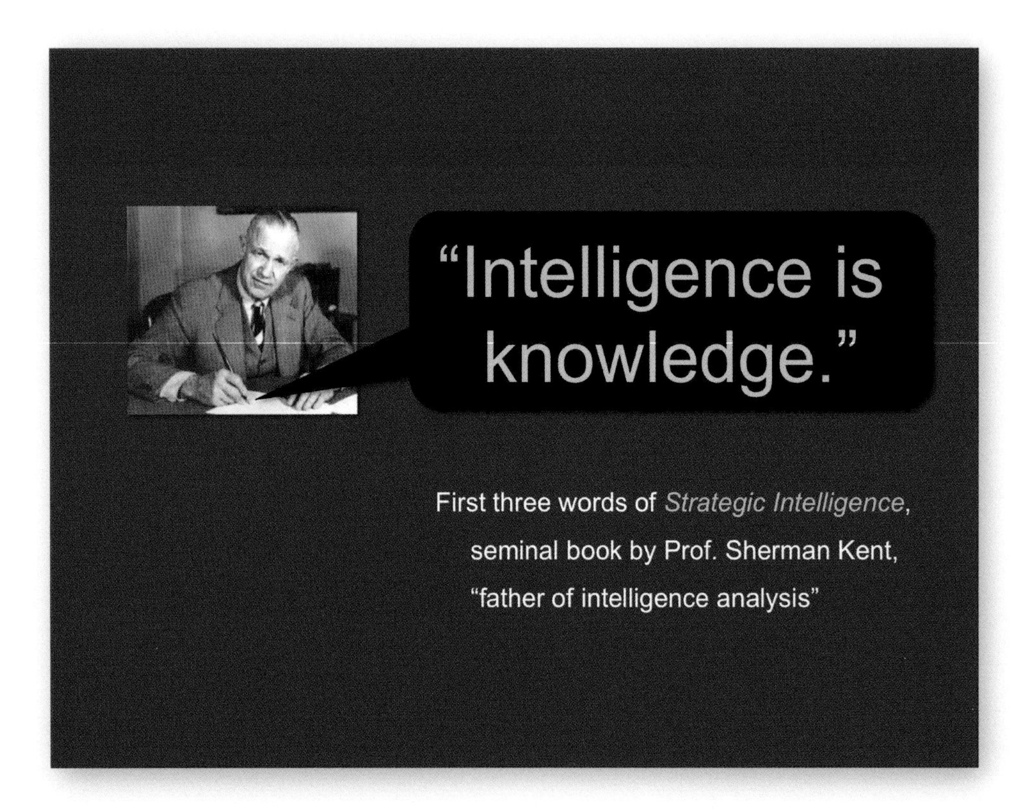

When we say *knowledge value chain*, this includes *intelligence,* too. In fact, the first three words of one of the first—and still among the greatest—books on intelligence are, "Intelligence is knowledge." The book was *Strategic Intelligence* by Sherman Kent.

Kent was a Yale history professor who took a leave of absence to help create the United States Central Intelligence Agency (CIA) in the late 1940s. He created many of the original concepts in intelligence analysis. Today the CIA's main training center is named after him.

The realization that intelligence is knowledge is not terribly useful, though—because not a whole lot is known in a rigorous way about the characteristics of knowledge as an economic resource. Though many of us would agree that most modern economies are now based on knowledge, we are just at the beginning of our understanding of how knowledge works best as a resource. I hope this book will make at least a small contribution to that immense and important effort.

Though occasionally I use the terms "knowledge" and "intelligence" interchangeably, I believe there are important and useful distinctions between them. We'll explore these later.

My Goals

- Help you learn to identify intelligence challenges
- Help you learn to find solutions
- Raise your intelligence ROI
- Avoid business and intelligence jargon
  - And explain it where we can't

I want to help you identify and solve your intelligence problems, issues, and challenges. This will help you raise your ROI on intelligence.

What I am going to show you here will seem simple, but it has been developed over the course of hundreds of intelligence projects I've conducted and/or led over the course of working with more than 100 corporate and government clients during the past four decades.

When you first start doing research, all projects seem unique—and, at some level, they are. But eventually the structural similarities among projects become apparent. Once you understand these common structures, you'll gain tremendous leverage in planning and executing each individual intelligence assignment.

The KVC is my attempt to distill these similarities down to a template that you can use to manage any intelligence or knowledge project, product, or process. I call it "the DNA of intelligence," because from these relatively simple building blocks, you can create an intelligence process of virtually any scope and scale, on virtually any subject.

Like many intelligence users, I am by training an MBA. I often find it convenient to use MBA-speak to describe things—for me, it's shorthand for the way things work. When I do that, however, I'll explain what I mean so that a smart layperson can understand and use the information.

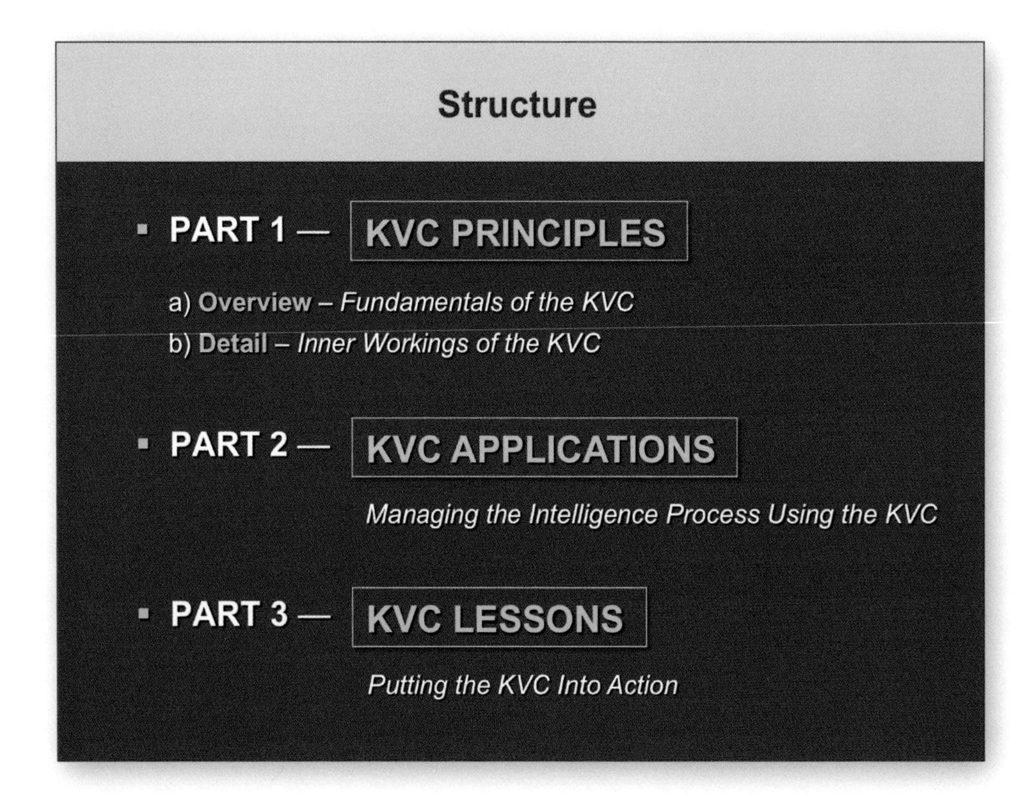

The KVC Clinic has three sections: *Principles, Applications,* and *Lessons*. We'll keep that structure for this handbook.

First we'll review *Principles*, which includes the theory behind the KVC model. Then we'll cover practice, reviewing some of the *Applications* that we have used with clients and that have been suggested by others.

By that point, you'll be able to apply the KVC to your own challenges, as presented in the *Lessons* section. If your organization is hosting a KVC Clinic, we conduct group exercises, typically on the second day of a two-day clinic.

If you're a stand-alone book user, you still can use the book to solve your own challenges. The Appendix contains a *Scorecard* that enables you to self-test for KVC improvements.

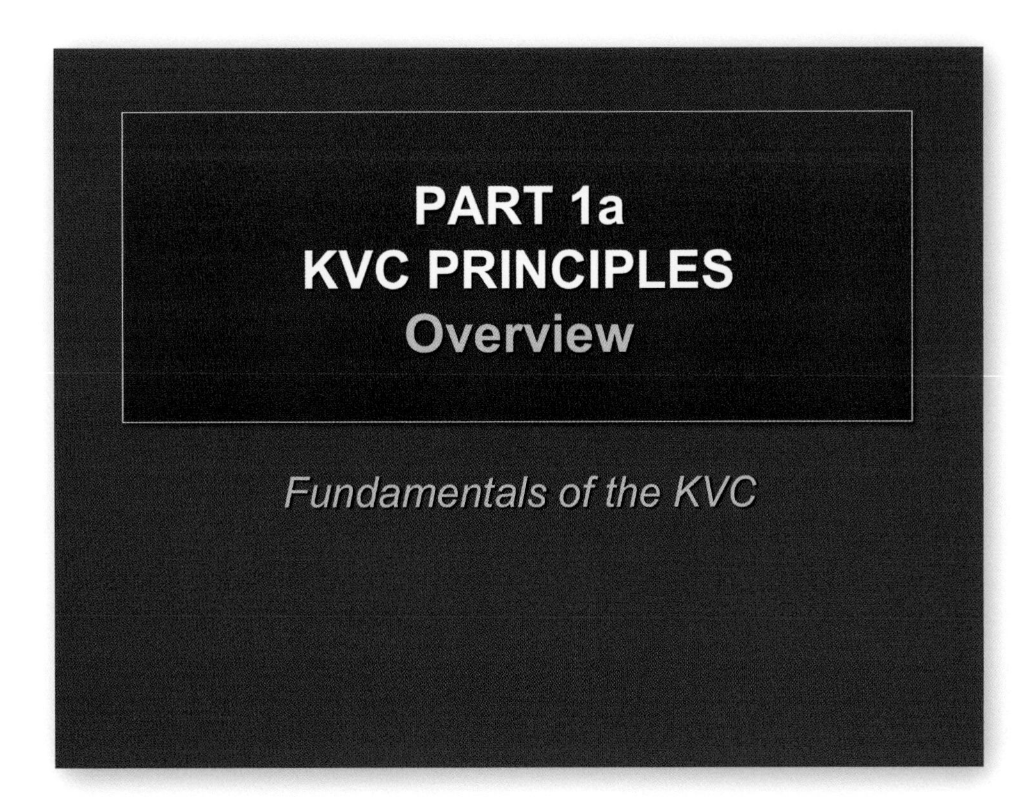

Principles contains an *Overview* and a *Details* section. In this ***Overview***, we'll explain the roots of the KVC model in Total Quality Management—the insight that, if you build quality into each stage of a process, quality is assured for the whole process. We'll look at how ROI is defined, and the many ways in which value is measured. We'll advocate for aligning intelligence metrics as closely as possible with the metrics of the business activities it supports.

We'll see how economic decisions are made under conditions of extreme uncertainty, and what role intelligence can play in reducing that uncertainty. We'll consider both the strategic and tactical scales of decision making.

We'll look briefly at *discounted cash flow*, which is an approach essential for understanding economic value. We'll look at cost-value trade-offs, and offer a way to think about the *marginal value* of data. We'll find out what a *value chain* is, and how it can be used to analyze knowledge work.

We'll introduce the KVC model, using illustrations from real-world business situations. Finally, we'll compare the KVC to other process models, including the government intelligence community's *intelligence cycle* and John Boyd's *OODA loops*.

"Physician, heal thyself." These words remind us that any discipline can benefit from taking its own medicine. Lawyers should obey the law, the shoemaker's children must have shoes, and so on.

The same is true for intelligence. If the discipline's tools are worth using at all, they are worth using on the discipline itself.

Every so often, we need to step back and take a fundamental look at how we conduct and manage knowledge processes. This will keep our approaches fresh as the needs of our clients evolve.

"What you would manage, first you must document." In order to manage or optimize the intelligence process, we will need to first *understand* it. In order to understand it, a necessary first step is to *document* it.

During the late 20th century, Edwards Deming and others developed the idea that to insure quality in manufacturing, you must embed it into the fiber of the process. The alternative—to just overlay it at the end of the process—is both ineffective and overly costly. The resulting quality revolution led to the development of tools like Total Quality Management (TQM), Business Process Management (BPM), and Six Sigma.

We'll apply that same basic approach in discussing intelligence and other knowledge-based processes, with the goal of increasing the ROI of intelligence.

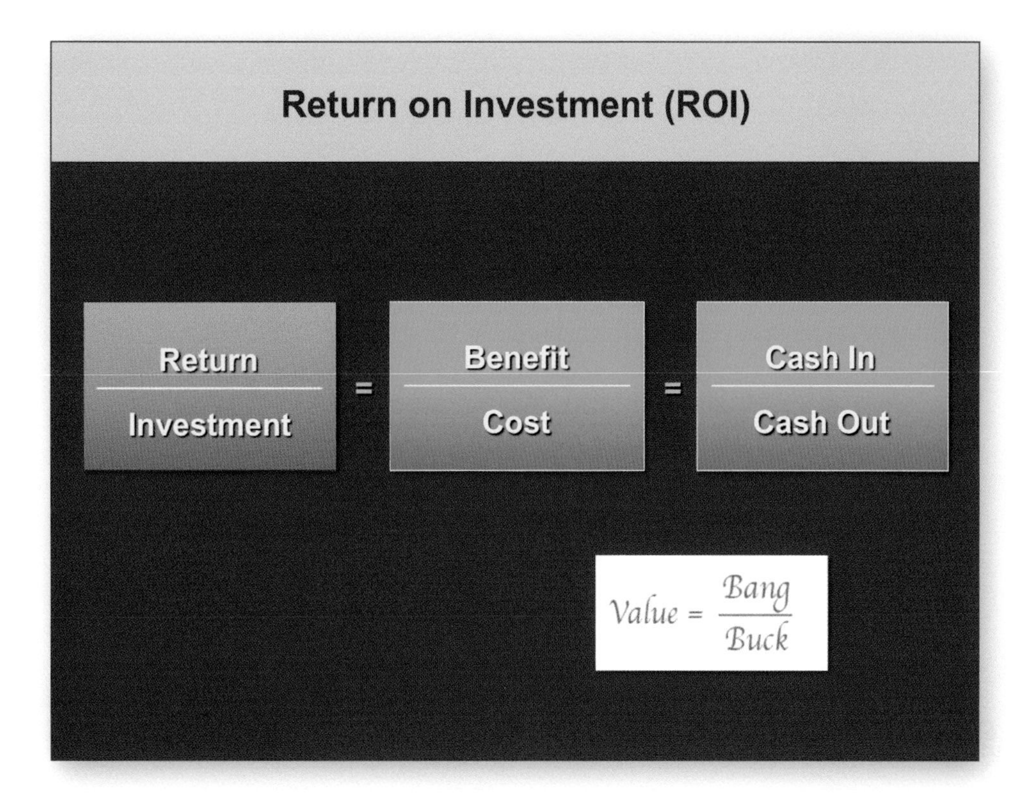

A good intelligence professional knows that the hidden assumptions are usually the ones that get us into trouble. One assumption about intelligence is that it is a *cost*—bottom-line, not top-line.

I want you to question this assumption. I want you to begin to see intelligence as an ***investment***, much like any other investment. You invest money into a stock today, you plan to sell it a year from now, and you will want to have gained a ***return*** in the interim.

If you're an intelligence producer, your clients invest in intelligence—they hired you, they pay for you to go to training and workshops, they hire outside firms that work as intelligence "out-sources," and so on.

What return do they get on this investment? How do they measure it? Are there goals you are expected to meet? How are these communicated?

The math of ROI is easy. *Return on investment* literally means net return divided by net investment. Another way of saying it: benefit divided by cost (though it's usually written *cost/benefit*).

Cash flow is often used as a measure of ROI, where the metrics are cash flow in and cash flow out. We'll discuss the *time value of money* later (p. 38).

In the vernacular, ROI is spoken of as ***value***—what you get for a given outlay. The American slang is "bang for the buck."

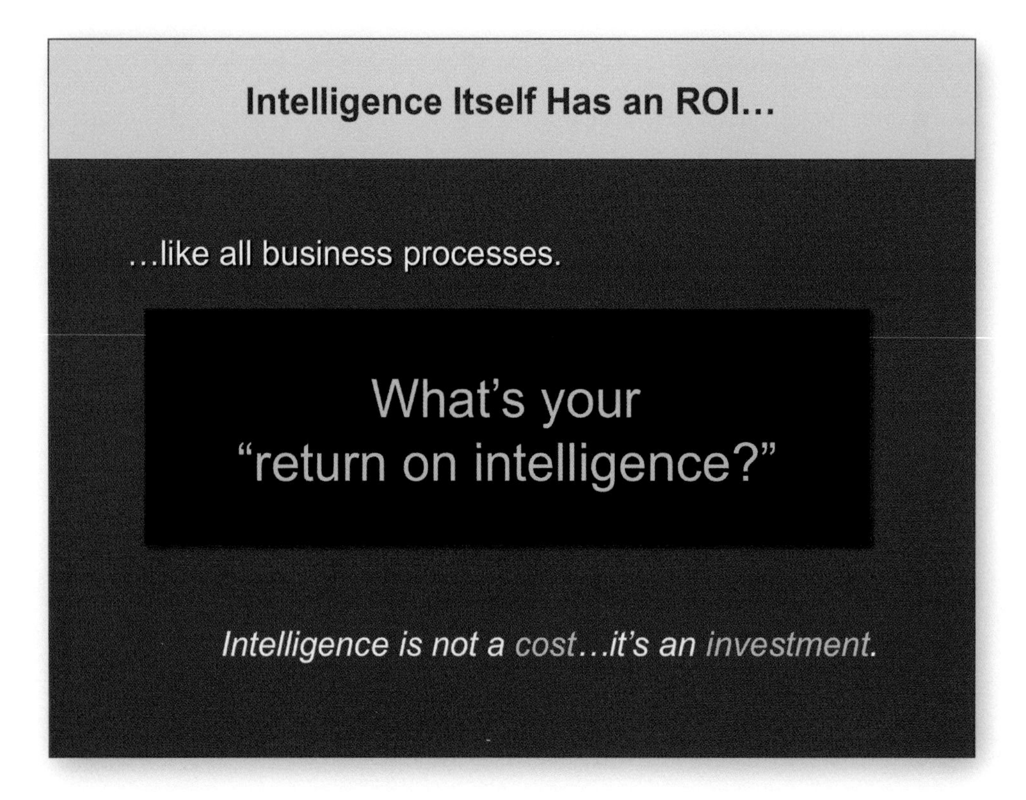

Each process in your business has an ROI, whether or not it is formally measured. Intelligence is a business process—and it too has an ROI.

TKA uses the motto "Intelligence is not a cost...it's an investment" to raise the expectation in our clients that they receive a fair return for their investments in intelligence.

As we said, the math of ROI is easy. But to accurately define—let alone measure—what a user benefit is can be problematic. There are many contributing factors and many processes working together simultaneously, and it's often hard to isolate the contribution of one from the contribution of another.

In the following pages we'll give you ways to focus on and even measure the value added by intelligence.

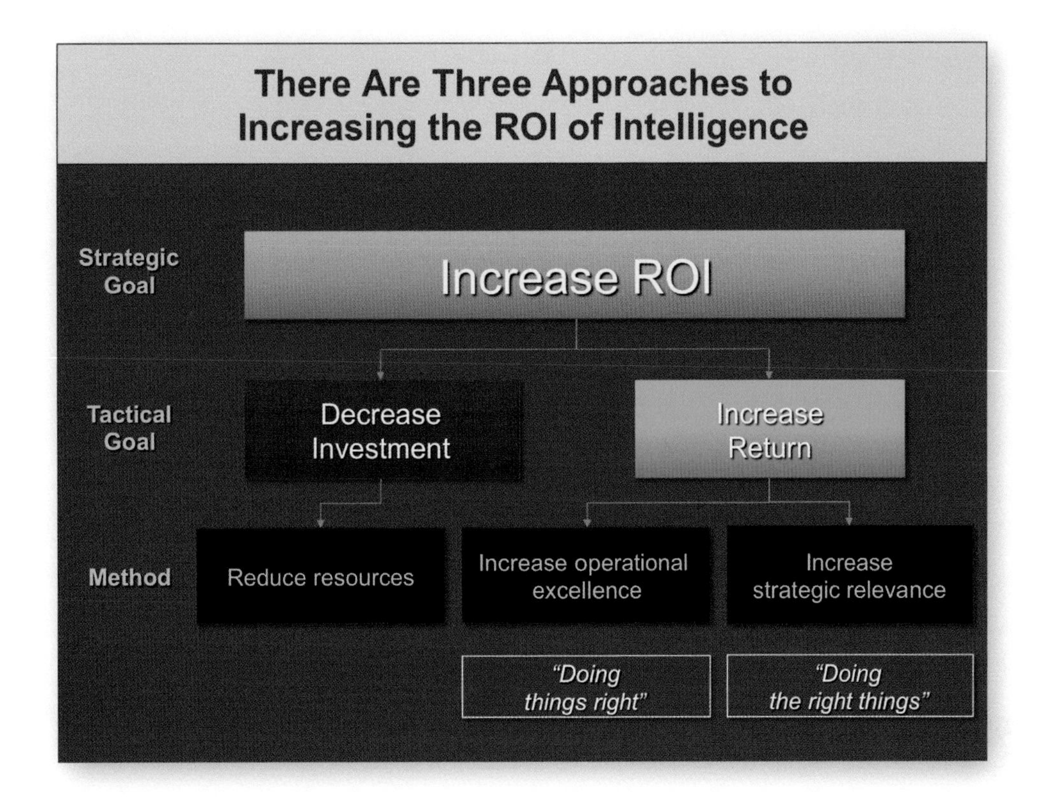

Because ROI is a ratio, there are only two fundamental ways to increase the overall ratio: decrease the bottom (the investment), or increase the top (the return). It's that simple.

Decreasing intelligence investment is especially straightforward—just call your office this afternoon, and tell them you resign. Bingo; you just saved your organization your salary.

Actually, that's not a good solution because (let's hope) you know what you are doing. Your firm would have to recruit another person, then train him—or even worse, hire one of those expensive contractors—so this would likely increase their net cost.

I was joking about resigning, of course—but am quite serious when I say that if managers are left to see intelligence as overhead cost (rather than investment), their most obvious ROI choice is to cut staffing and other outlays. And this does happen. In fact, seeing this happen many times under many conditions in many types of clients is partly what prompted me to develop the KVC model.

You can learn to do things *more effectively*, or *more efficiently*, or—and this is what we'll aim for—*both*. We'll call this ***operational excellence***, or "doing things right." In effect, this increases the top of the ROI equation—the return or value received.

There is another powerful way to increase return—***strategic relevance***, or "doing the right things." Unless you have an unlimited intelligence budget, you'll need to focus your resources at the points where they create the greatest return. In effect, this brings intelligence into alignment with business strategy—an improvement that typically has an even bigger impact on ROI than doing things right.

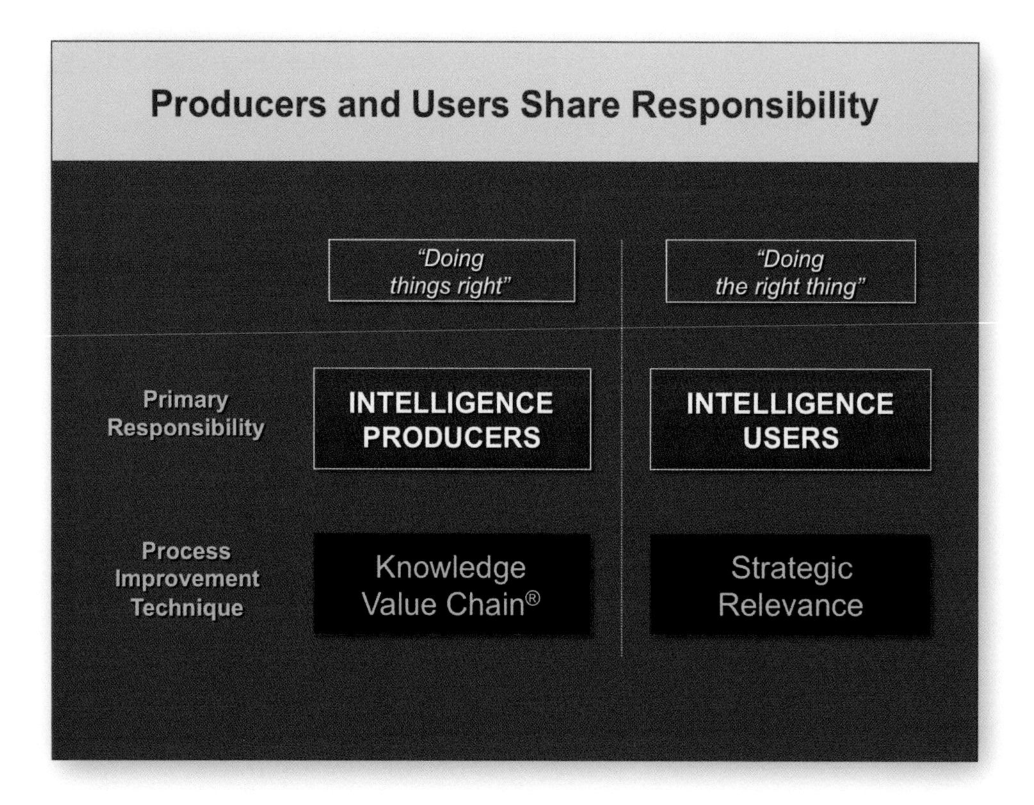

"Doing things right" is what producers can control, and what the Knowledge Value Chain is intended to address.

"Doing the right things" is nominally the job of the people who manage and/or use intelligence. Intelligence producers are often *tasked* to do things; they do not write their own intelligence assignments and directives.

However, intelligence producers can and should play a more active role in determining research needs and agendas than they typically do. We call the goal of such initiatives ***strategic relevance.***

Strategic relevance will help you now to understand your intelligence client—and will help you in the future if you evolve into an intelligence manager and/or user role.

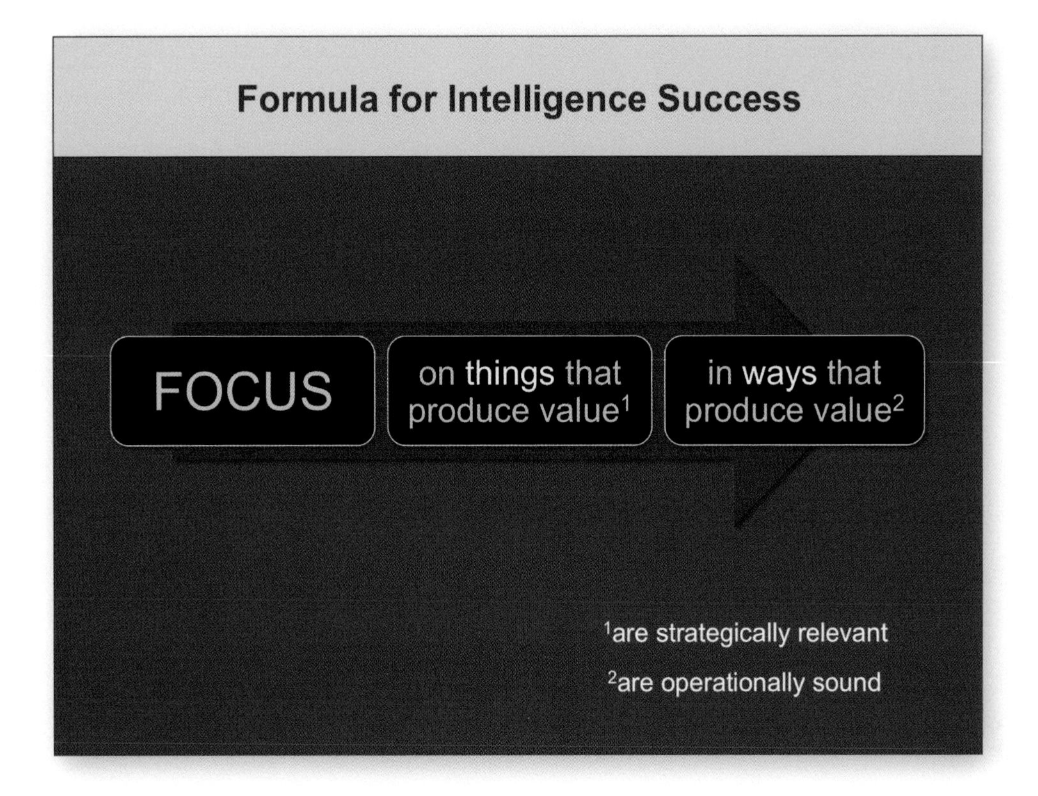

We have consistently found that executives in a range of roles are overwhelmed by the amounts of data being continually directed their way. *Data overload* is a problem that is here to stay. The intelligence professional should be aware of this, and help ameliorate it—instead of adding to the growing cacophony.

Here's a simple mantra to remind you of the dual goals of operational excellence and strategic relevance: **Focus on *things* that produce value** (i.e., that are strategically relevant) **in *ways* that produce value** (i.e., that are operationally excellent.)

CASE EXAMPLE

A corporate strategy executive with whom I had worked for several years challenged me one day. "Tim, we ask you and your team to get lots of information for us, and you do it well; but can you tell us what really matters? What do we need to pay closest attention to?"

We built a model for him of the 15 strategic factors having the greatest impact on his business. We also developed descriptions and metrics of how they were changing over time, and proposed actions to manage them.

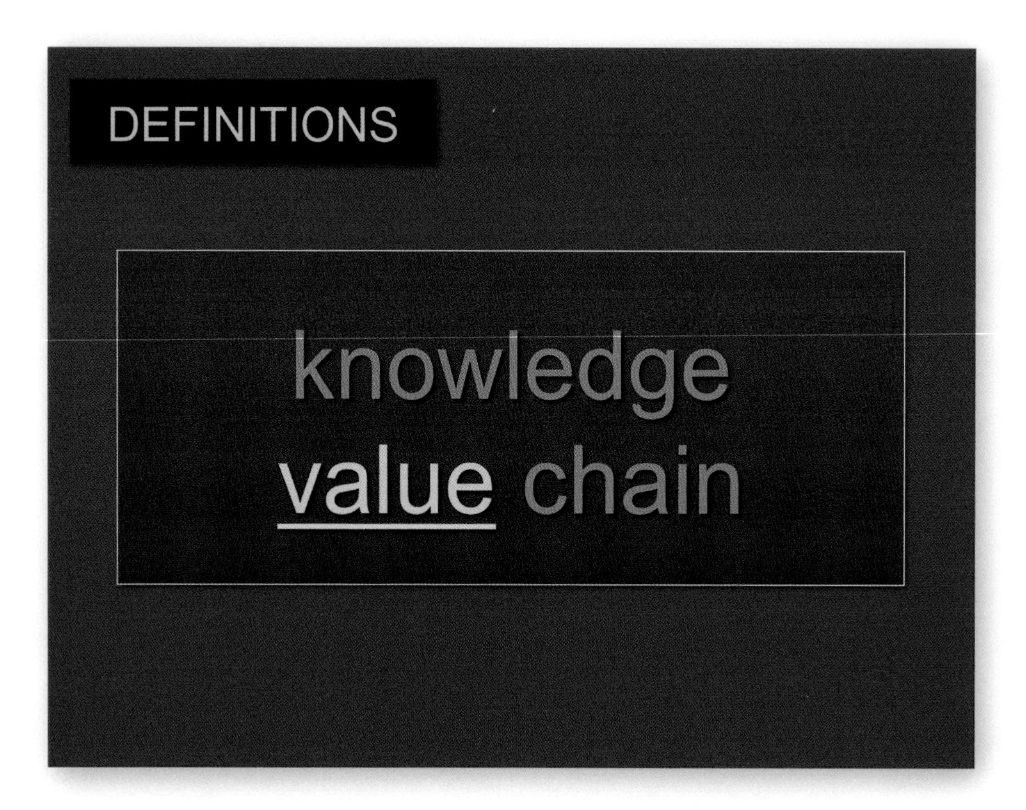

I've shifted from talking about *return on investment* to talking about *value*. It's time to back up and get some definitions.

Once during a workshop I was asked, "What is the difference between 'value' and 'values'?" It's a subtle distinction. Merriam-Webster defines *value* as "a fair return or equivalent in goods, services, or money for something exchanged." *Values* is defined as "principles or qualities [held] intrinsically valuable or desirable."

It's the former sense—economic value—that we're focused on here. Our research shows that as many half of all KVC problems originate from its Value step. Understanding how value is defined and produced is a key to understanding corrections and improvements in the rest of the knowledge or intelligence process.

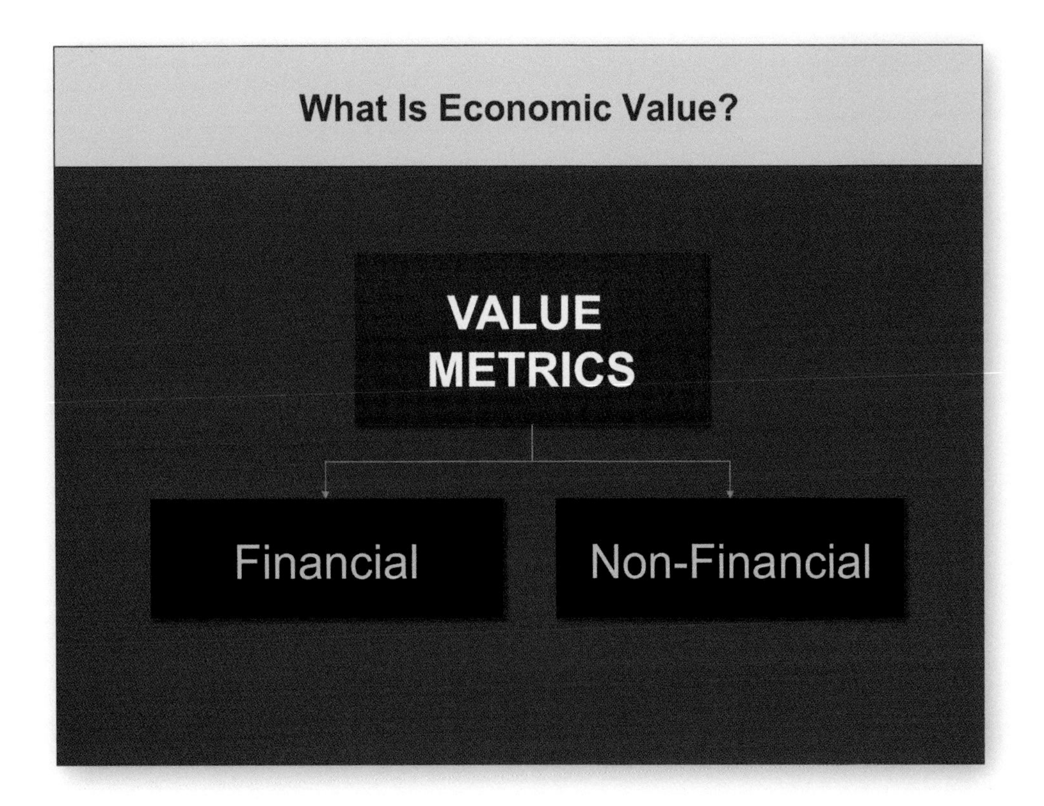

More specifically, we're focusing on the kind of economic value you can measure. Companies often focus on ***financial*** metrics, since for publicly-traded companies these are most often what matter to management and investors. But companies have lately discovered there are ***non-financial*** indicators that are also worth measuring rigorously.

The following section on value and how it is measured will help you:

- **Understand the user perspective.** It's crucial to understand how your client views her business problem and its potential impact on value. These will give you insight in how best to serve her needs.
- **Understand how intelligence is judged.** The *value-relevance* of your work will serve as the basis for how your client evaluates the intelligence product and process, whether formally or informally.
- **Understand competitive dynamics.** In doing competitive research, you must cultivate an awareness of those things that will produce value for your organization (*opportunities*) and those that will cause value to be impaired or destroyed (*threats*). It's not enough to know what actions a rival is undertaking or planning—you need to also understand the *value impact* that these actions will potentially have on your organization.

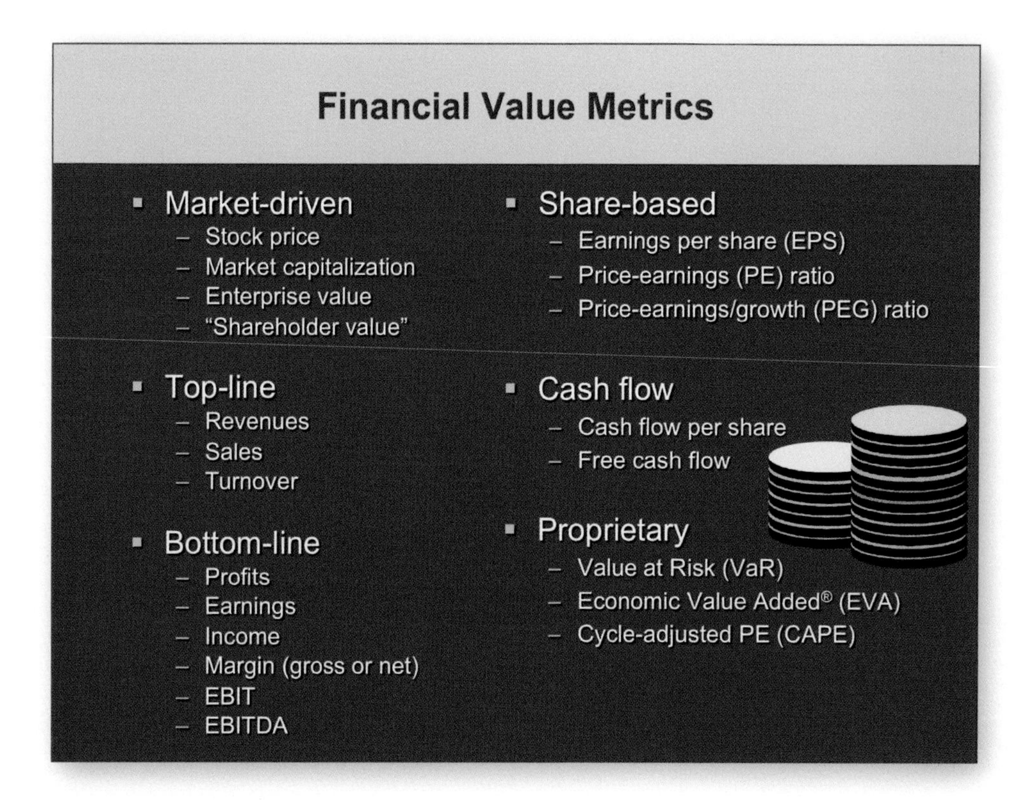

There are many definitions of measurable economic value. This slide lists those used most frequently, and categorizes them by approach.

Many of these metrics use market value (stock price, or shareholder value) as a starting point. For traded companies, this single consensus number reflects, in real time, all the available knowledge and opinion about each company and its competitive situation, with inputs from hundreds of experts, and reflects what is known about future trends that may affect the company.

Financial metrics may seem like eternal truths, but in fact have their own life cycle—they are created, come into fashion, and go out of fashion. Over time, financial markets change their ways of looking at value, and financial academics and journalists find new and improved ways of thinking about it.

For example, the *Price/Earnings ratio* is a quick measure of whether a stock is overvalued, undervalued, or fairly valued. This ratio's traditional earnings time frame is one year. As such the ratio is sensitive to fluctuations in earnings, which can vary widely over the business cycle of growth and recession. Prof. Robert Shiller of Yale has championed a *cyclically-adjusted P/E* (CAPE) ratio that reduces these cyclical fluctuations by measuring earnings over a longer time frame (like ten years). This is seen by some as a more stable and reliable metric than the classic P/E.

Non-Financial Value Metrics

- Market share
- Quality
  - Six Sigma
- Innovation
  - Number of patents
- Customer satisfaction
- Brand value
  - Interbrand
- Intangibles
- Key performance indicators (KPIs)
- Balanced scorecard
  - Kaplan and Norton

Interbrand

It has become clear that, while there are many closely watched financial metrics, there are also non-financial indicators that can—and should—be rigorously measured and monitored. These lead indirectly to value in the economic sense. Market share is an obvious one, because it's an important signal of where a company stands strategically.

Quality and customer satisfaction measures are also important, and are now routinely collected and analyzed by most companies.

Because we are now living in a *knowledge economy*, there are more tools available to measure *intellectual capital*—for example, the value of patents, the rate of innovation, and the value of brands and other intangible assets.

Key performance indicators (KPI) are important internally, and may also be watched by external analysts.

Many now believe that a company needs a *balanced scorecard* that reports multiple dimensions of performance. Such non-financial metrics systems are widely used.

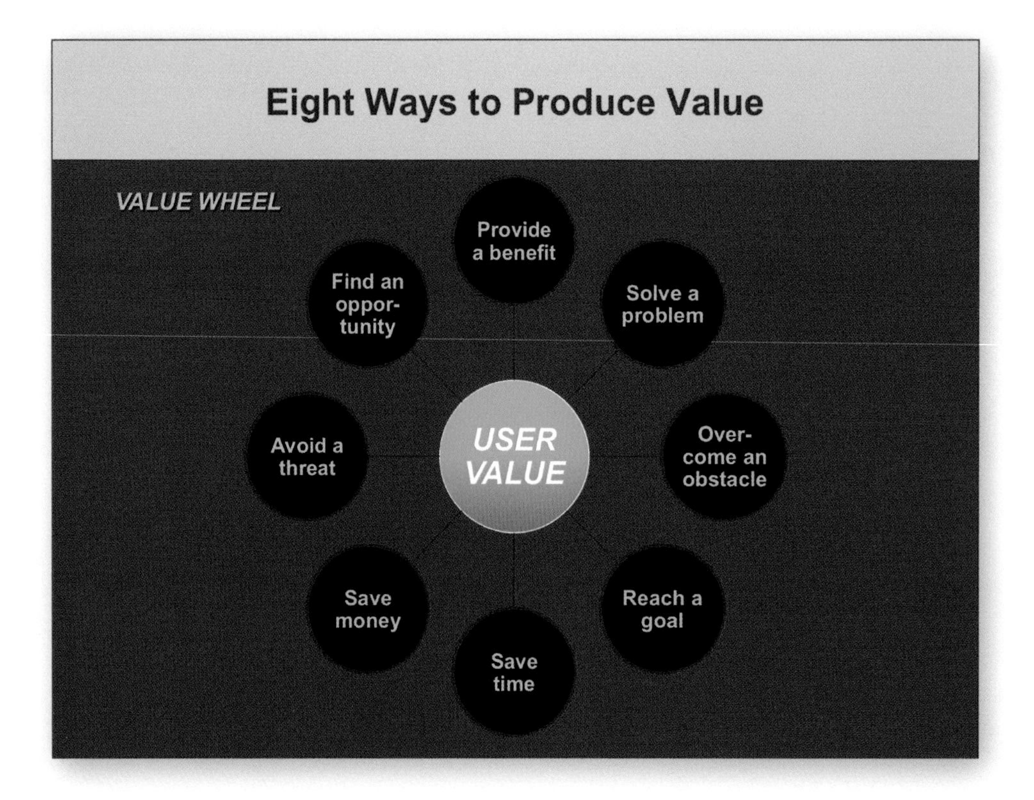

In everyday terms, what is value? We use this ***value wheel*** to describe eight fundamental ways to produce value. We provide a benefit; solve somebody's problem; help them overcome an obstacle or reach a goal; save them time or money; or help them avoid a threat or find an opportunity.

There may be others, or variations on these, but we find this a good place to start. In providing effective intelligence or other knowledge services—or any other business service or product, for that matter—you should find yourself on or near one of these goals.

Intelligence producers are often trained to go to their client users and ask, "What kind of information do you want or need?" This is well-intentioned, but usually not effective in my experience. It is not the intelligence user's job to know what intelligence she needs.

A more productive approach is to ask, "What business challenges do you have? What keeps you awake at night?" A competent intelligence professional will know which aspects of his clients' problems can be solved using intelligence—and how to do that.

A problem solved creates a satisfied client of the intelligence process and its practitioner— and as such is a high-ROI experience.

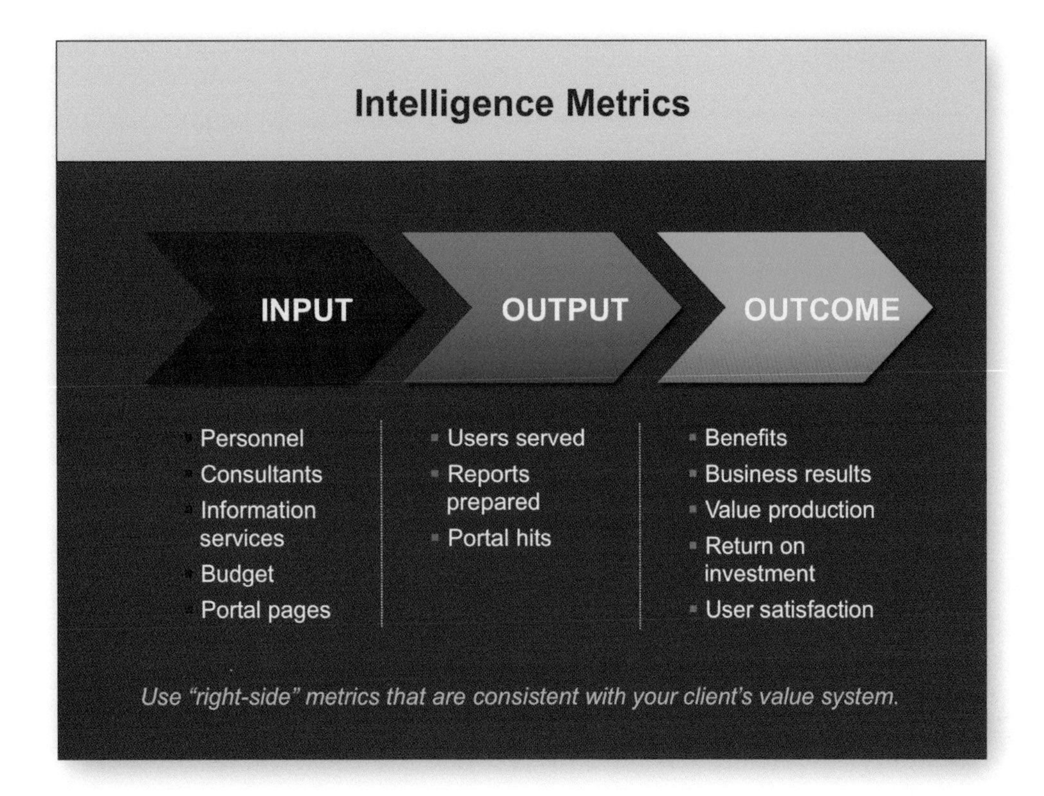

Here's a way to think about the different kinds of metrics that could be applied to intelligence or other knowledge work. This approach differentiates among measures of Input, Output, and Outcome.

Inputs are the resources that we invest in the intelligence process. These are typically things that involve budget outlays: personnel, consultants, information services, portal pages, and so on.

Outputs are the near-term results of those outlays, such as number of intelligence users served, number of reports prepared, or hits on our intelligence portal. These things are relatively easy to measure, and form the basis of a typical metrics-based knowledge productivity system.

Outputs, however, don't measure what we are really trying to achieve, which is the net business result of our activities—the ***Outcomes***. They include things like greater sales, greater profits, and greater competitiveness in general.

Why don't we just directly measure outcomes? We don't, typically, because it's difficult to attribute outcomes on a cause-and-effect basis. Increased sales, for example, could be due in part to an effective sales intelligence process, but almost certainly also has other causal factors.

Often we use metrics that function as *proxies* for outcomes. Intelligence user satisfaction, as measured by ongoing feedback and small surveys, is probably the most common of these.

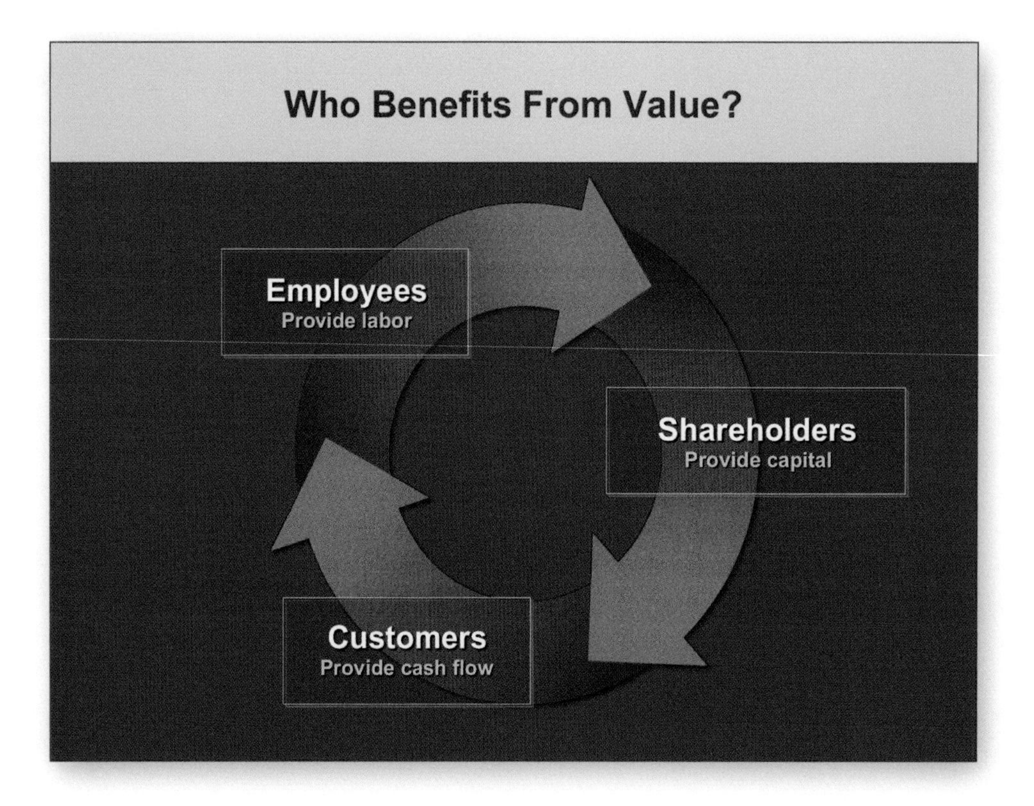

When we speak of the value created by intelligence, whose benefit do we mean? There are three primary kinds of stakeholders for whom value is produced by intelligence and other knowledge processes.

Shareholder value comes most readily to mind, since investors provide the capital that make the enterprise run. Shareholder value (or return on equity) is the way we measure how investors are compensated for the use of that capital.

Other stakeholders benefit too. ***Customers*** provide cash flow by buying our products and services. In a very real sense, customers finance our intelligence operations. Therefore it is reasonable to think they should benefit directly from our enhanced competitiveness—as they do through product innovations, lower prices, better service, and so on.

Employees, including contractors, provide labor for the enterprise, and they too benefit. A more competitive enterprise is better able to provide livelihoods and security for its employees.

The value needs of these groups may align or may be in conflict. When profits rise, for example, shareholders may seek higher dividends, customers may seek lower prices, and employees may seek higher wages and benefits.

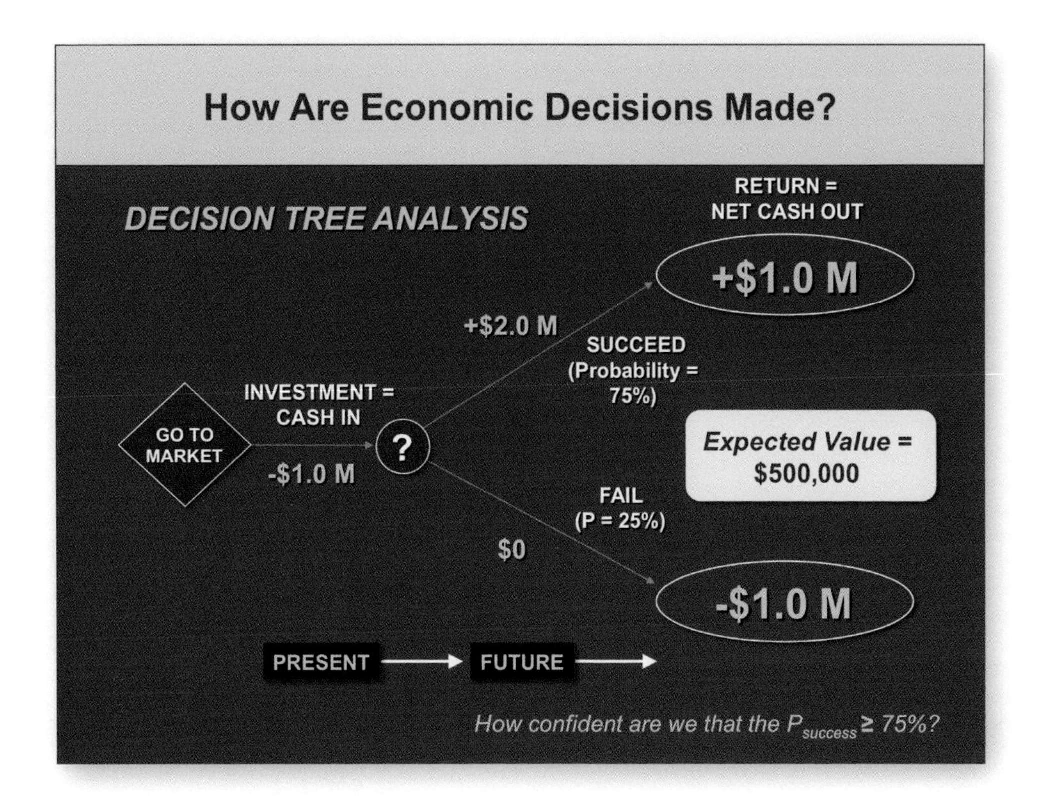

How do your decision maker/clients look at value? It's possible they have been trained to use *decision trees*. Whether or not they use this technique formally, it's a way of thinking that—once you know it—becomes fundamental to the ways you assess value.

Business decisions are like the game of poker. You place bets about the future (strategic investments) based on incomplete information about the other players' cards (the external business environment). You make high-stakes decisions where (1) the future is unknown and unknowable in any meaningful sense, and (2) you're dealing with partial and imperfect information, even about events that have already occurred.

Decision tree analysis is a way of managing around the doubly imperfect information we have about the future. Here's a simple example.

Let's say you have a chance to bring a new product to market. The market launch will require a cash outlay estimated at $1 million, regardless of whether or not the product succeeds. Your informed assumption is that if the product succeeds, it will bring in cash of $2 million—a net gain of $1 million. If, on the other hand, it fails, it will bring in nothing—a net loss of $1 million.

You know (or assume) that your probability of success is 75%, and of failure is 25%. Given those assumptions, your *expected value* of the launch is [.75×(1.0M) + .25×(-1.0M)], or $500,000. Without better information about your assumptions, that is the net amount you are predicted to gain from the product introduction.

Intelligence can play a major role in sharpening these estimates of value and probability.

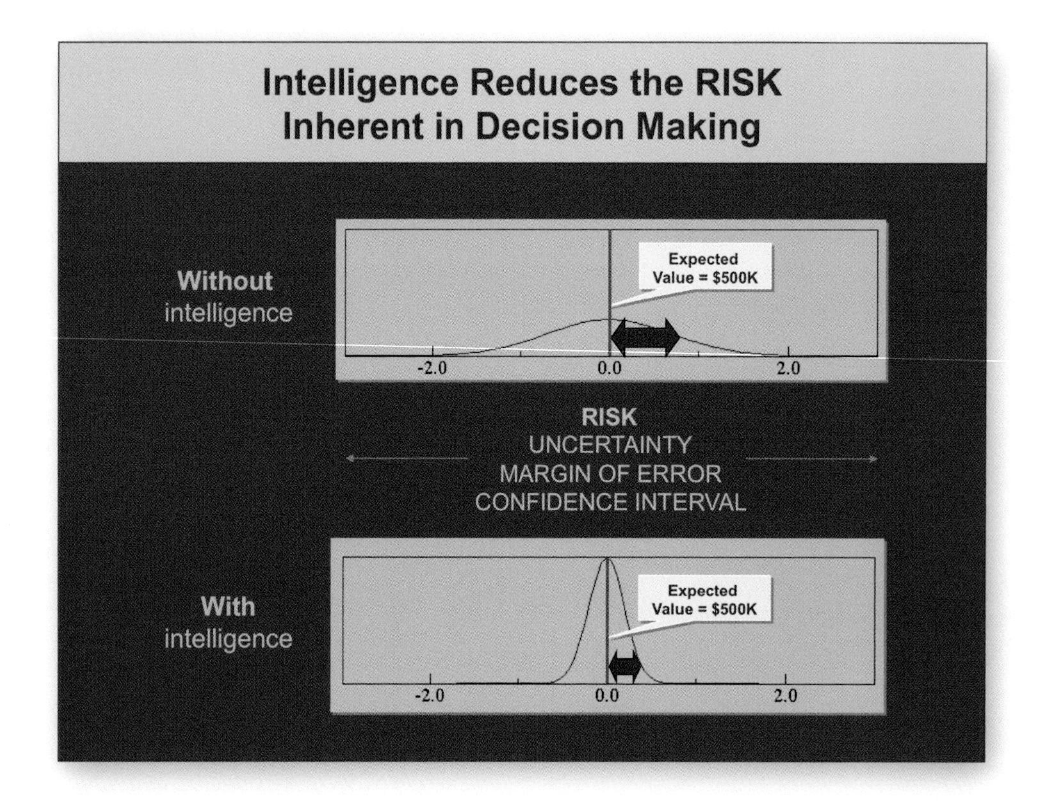

The concept of ***risk*** is widely misunderstood to mean something bad—a threat. As we use it here, risk is a statistical function that describes the potential variability of an expected outcome. There is upside risk (i.e., opportunity) and downside risk (i.e., threat).

Statisticians describe risk by *standard deviations*—but most of us know it as ***uncertainty, margin of error***, or ***confidence interval***. It basically measures the surprise factor—the *reliability* of a forecast about a future outcome or other unknown.

Intelligence cannot reliably predict the future—no mere mortal can do that. What intelligence can and should do is reduce the surprise factor by *narrowing the band of risk* within which a potential future outcome falls. A narrower risk band implies a higher probability that what you *expect* to happen, *does* happen. In this way, intelligence helps to manage risk by allowing your business to plan for unforeseen and unknowable circumstances.

Some people call this "making better decisions"— but it's significantly more than that. Effectively managing strategic risk increases the economic value and competitiveness of the enterprise over time.

Risk management is not always governed by perfect rationality. Studies have shown that most people are *loss-averse*—we prefer avoiding a downside risk (loss) over gaining a financially equivalent upside risk (gain). People hate losing more than they love winning.

Two Scales of Decision

	STRATEGIC	TACTICAL
TIME FRAME	Longer	Shorter
VALUE AT RISK ("Stakes")	Greater	Smaller
LEVEL IN THE ENTERPRISE	Executive Management	Operating Management
EXAMPLE PROBLEM	"What business(es) should we be in?"	"How can we win this sale?"

Complementary and both essential

The terms ***strategic*** and ***tactical*** are often used in reference to decisions, and to the intelligence that supports these decisions. Like many things in business, this is occasionally a useful distinction, but rarely a black-or-white one. Many real-world decisions and actions fall on a continuum between the two and contain elements of each.

Generally speaking, a strategic decision involves a commitment of greater resources ("stakes") over a longer period of time than a tactical one. As such, strategic decisions are weighed more carefully, by more people, and at a higher level in the organization, than are tactical ones.

There is a mutually supportive relationship between strategy and tactics. Without great tactics, great strategies cannot succeed. Conversely, tactics that are not guided by strategies can become random and uncoordinated, and consequently ineffective.

"What business(es) should we be in?" is the essential strategy question proposed by Peter Drucker. "How can we win this sale?" is a typical tactical question. Both kinds of questions must be answered optimally for the enterprise to thrive, and both should be supported by intelligence proportional to the *value at risk*—i.e., the potential cost of a wrong answer.

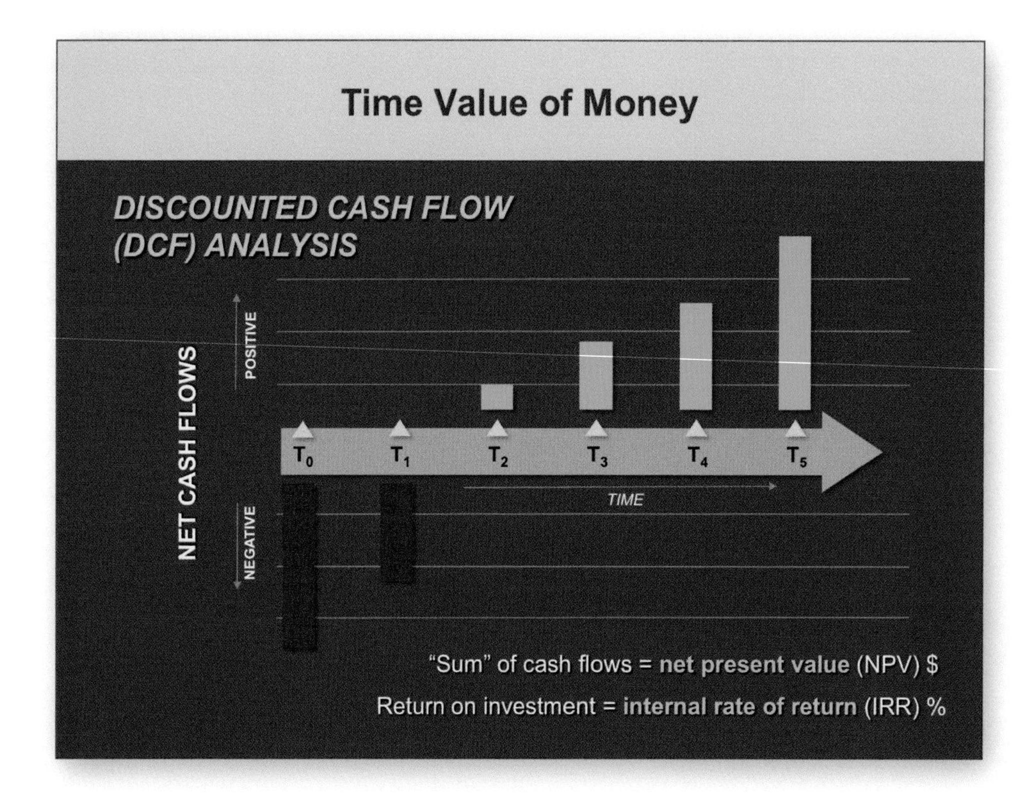

Any discussion of value in the business world should include some reference to the ***time value of money***. This is described formally by ***discounted cash flow*** *(DCF)* analysis, and is also known by its mathematical representations, ***net present value*** *(NPV)* and ***internal rate of return*** *(IRR)*.

The *time value of money* means that if you invest (wisely) a dollar today, it will be worth more than that tomorrow, still more the next day, and so on. Its value increases over time.

Conversely, a dollar you receive today is worth more than a dollar you will receive tomorrow, because (at least in theory) you could invest it overnight and earn some interest. So by tomorrow, you should have a little more than a dollar. And there is always a small chance that tomorrow's anticipated dollar won't be there at all by tomorrow.

In the real world, financial returns are rarely received in a lump sum as in our decision tree example (p. 35)—they are earned over time. In the simple example above, we could invest now (negative cash flow at time 0, or T_0) and again a year from now (T_1), then show a little positive cash flow in year two (T_2), even more in year three (T_3), and so on.

Discounting the cash flows is a mathematical way of adjusting for the fact that we'll receive some of the return in the future—and that in the meantime, we will not yet have the investment use of those funds.

Strategic Events

- What events typically put the greatest "value at risk"?
  - New product introduction
  - New market entry
  - Facilities - build, buy, or close
  - Business acquisition or sale
  - Product acquisition or sale
  - New key hire

As mentioned earlier, the *strategic relevance* of intelligence is key to building its ROI (p. 25). Recall the first part of our intelligence success formula, "Focus on things that produce value...." This implies that in conducting intelligence, you should always follow the money. This will guide you to the right path much of the time.

Those same things that can produce significant value for your firm can erode your value if a direct rival initiates them. What are these?

Certain key kinds of competitor initiatives should *always* be scrutinized by intelligence. These are the events that put greatest value at risk by producing (or eroding) value.

When your own company undertakes any of these initiatives, intelligence analysis should be called on to support the decision. If these decisions are being made in your company without your analytic input, you have the opportunity to add greater value by getting involved in helping make them.

I estimate that more than 90% of the projects I've worked on as a strategy analyst over several decades have to do with one (or more) of these issues: a new product introduction or market entry; buying, building, or closing a facility (a manufacturing plant, for example); acquiring or selling a business or product line; or a key executive hire or promotion.

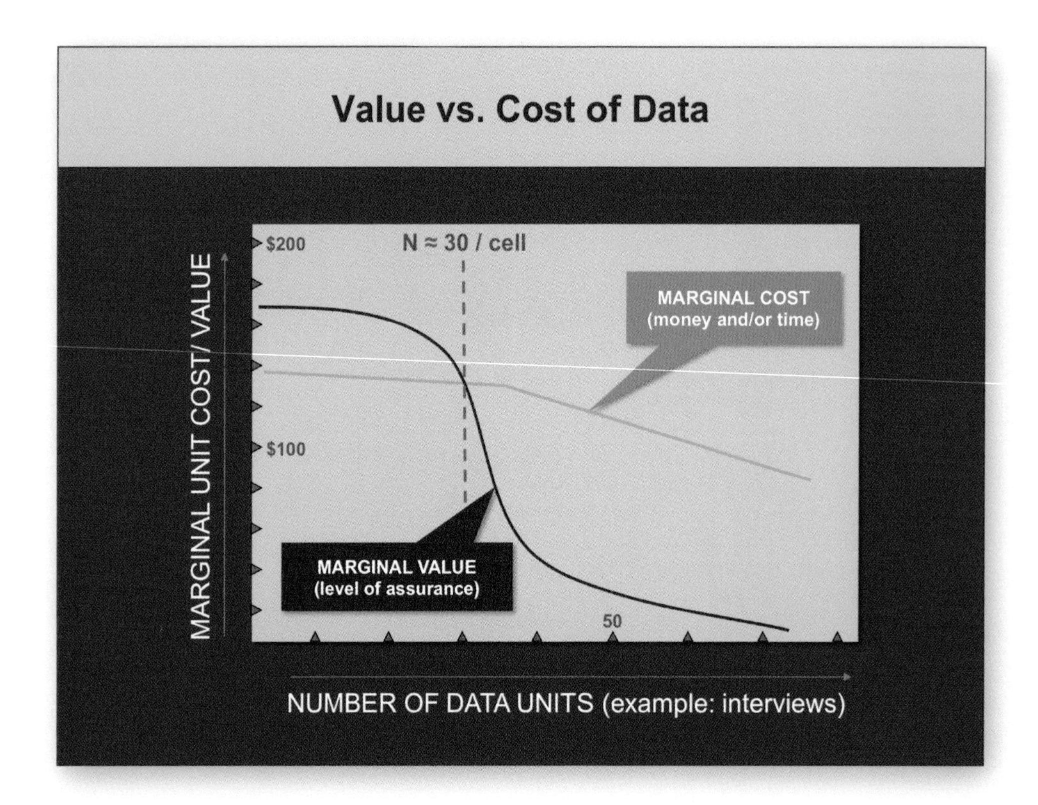

When we think of the value of something, it's convenient to think of its cost or price. This is both inaccurate and misleading. Cost and value are fundamentally different, and you must understand the distinction before you can raise ROI. Cost is what you pay; value is what you get in return—the "bang for the buck."

Economists use a concept called *marginal value* to describe how, if you spend more on something, you don't necessarily get proportionally more value for your money. For example, a $50,000 car by definition costs twice as much as a $25,000 car. But is it twice as valuable? Both get you where you want to go when you want to go there. The $50,000 car may have a nicer ride and overall user experience— but twice as nice? Possibly, but not likely.

The same is true in intelligence. You could spend twice as much money and/or time gathering data, yet not increase your knowledge of the subject by nearly that amount. For example, you could conduct 500 consumer interviews to learn whether consumers prefer a particular feature for your product. You could then conduct 500 more interviews—likely to cost nearly as much as the first 500—and still come out with much the same answer. You have doubled your cost, but not doubled your knowledge or understanding of the topic at hand.

A statistician would say that you will have decreased the *confidence interval* of your answer (see p. 36)—the likelihood that you are wrong. Technically, that is true—but to what extent, and is that added confidence in the answer worth the added cost?

>>

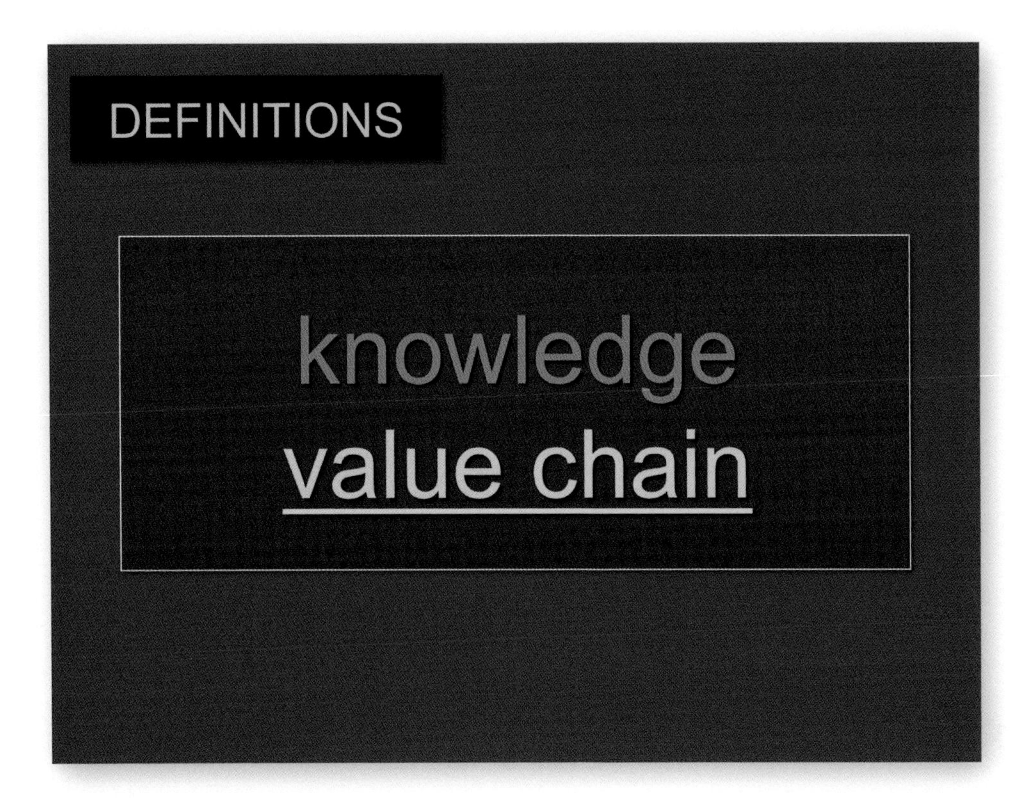

>>

There are always hidden, non-monetary costs in intelligence—*time*, for example. While you are gathering more data, the world is turning, and situations are evolving—sometimes rapidly.

Another hidden cost in intelligence is the *attention* of decision makers required to focus on the results. This is rarely factored in explicitly, and can be substantial due both to the high aggregate salary cost per hour of executive meetings and to the *opportunity cost* of what else they could be thinking about.

All that said, these points remain:

- Having *some* information is nearly always better than having none.
- You can never have *complete* or perfect information.
- Acquiring additional information always involves a *trade-off* between its marginal cost and its marginal value.

If you wait until you have all the relevant data, you will never be able to act—or produce value. The intelligence expert should be prepared to advise his client on the cost/value balance of any particular additional piece of intelligence.

OK, that's "value." Now what's a "value chain"?

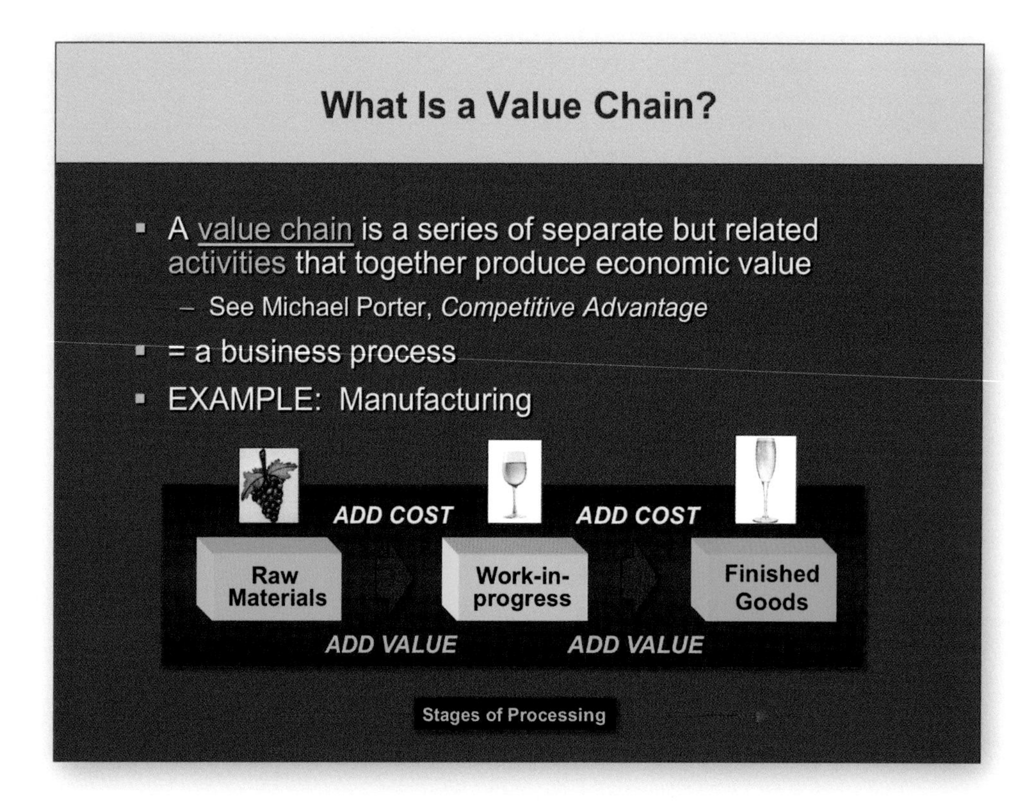

A ***value chain*** is a series of activities that together, in sequence, produce economic value. Manufacturing a product is a value chain. Let's take a fun product, champagne, for example. *Raw materials* (grapes) are processed to make a *work-in-progress* (stuff that is partly made, in this example white wine) and then converted into *finished goods* (the final product we buy, champagne.)

At each stage of processing, work is done to move he product to the next stage. Cost is added—labor, fuel, power, ingredients like sugar and yeast, etc.—and value is added.

Remember that cost and value are different (p. 40). Ideally, more value is produced at each stage than cost expended. If that is not true—especially in sum for the overall production chain—the ROI is negative. The process needs to be *re-engineered* by reducing costs and/or raising the value of the final product (by advertising the product more widely, for example.)

Why does champagne typically cost more per bottle than the component wine? Why does wine cost more than grapes?

It's partly that more resources (i.e., costs) have gone into making the former in each pair. But it's also because the former in each pair commands a greater value (i.e., price) in the marketplace.

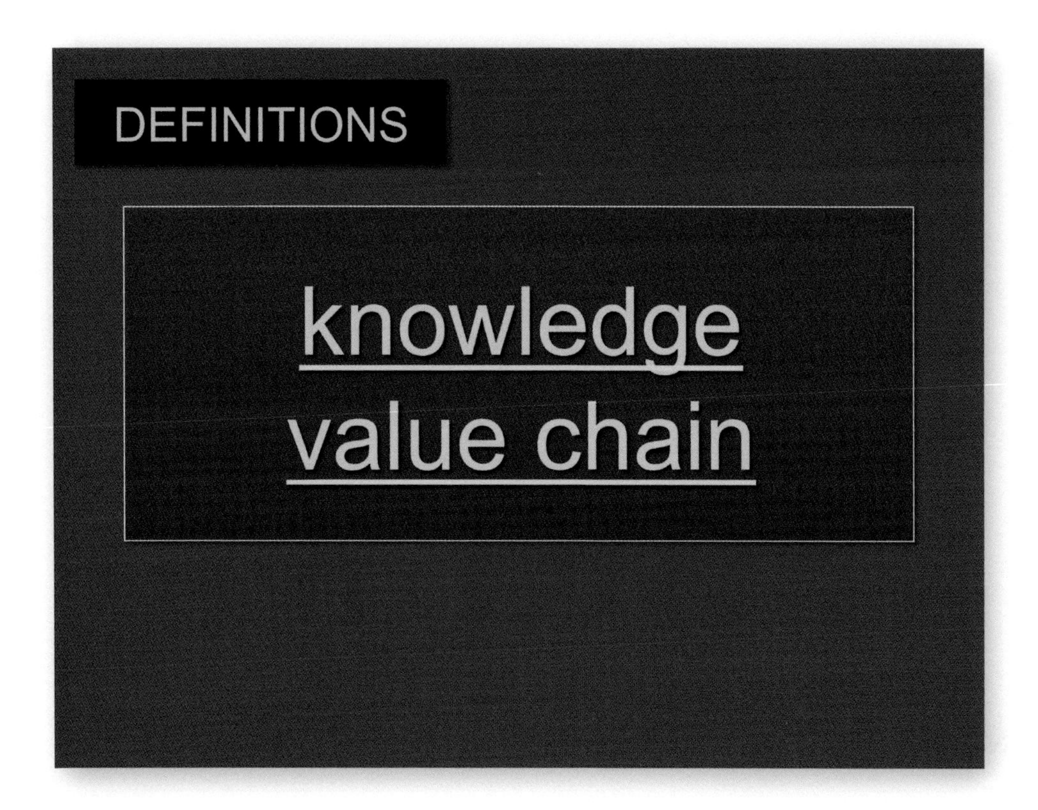

Our key premise is that turning data into information, then into knowledge, and then into intelligence is itself a manufacturing process. It can therefore be analyzed and improved like any other manufacturing process.

Economists who study information and knowledge typically focus on *differences* between traditional assets and knowledge assets. Knowledge assets are intangible that you can't see, touch, or feel. And knowledge assets are *non-rivalrous*—if I give you my information, I continue to have it, too.

I believe it's equally valid, and often more productive, to focus on the *similarities* between knowledge processing and the processing of material goods. This analogy yields many useful insights about the origins of, and solutions to, intelligence and knowledge challenges.

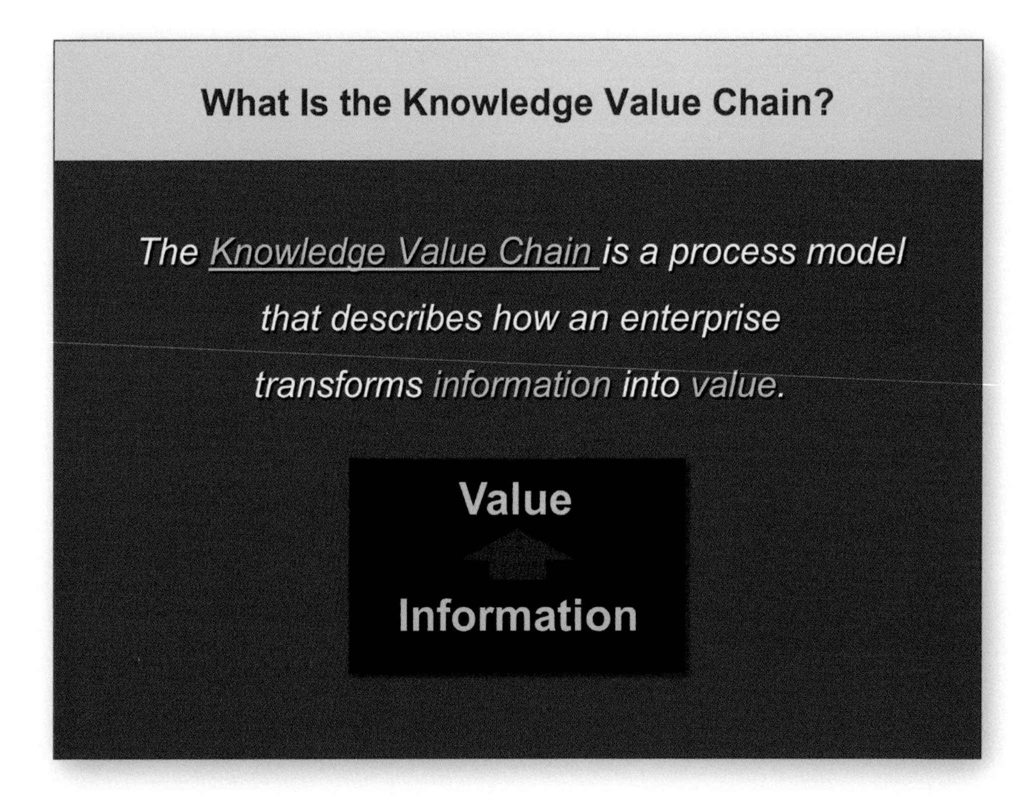

The Knowledge Value Chain® is a process model that describes how Data-Information-Knowledge-Intelligence—"DIKI"—are transformed into enterprise value. The KVC serves as the basis for a diagnostic and improvement methodology available from The Knowledge Agency®.

If we describe and document that process, we can understand it. If we understand it, we can improve upon it. If we improve upon it in one situation, we can improve on it in other, similar situations.

The KVC Model Can Be Applied to Any Knowledge-Based Activity, Including:

- Research libraries
- Competitive intelligence
- Market research
- Scientific research
- R&D (research and development)
- Investment due diligence
- Legal research

The KVC framework describes activities conducted in many professions, including scientific research, legal discovery, investment due diligence, and corporate intelligence. Though the terminology and content vary, the processes and pitfalls are similar at a fundamental level.

Mixing different knowledge-based parts of a client organization often stimulates productive energy and synergies. In KVC workshops and clinics, we've had R&D people sitting next to business strategists and corporate librarians.

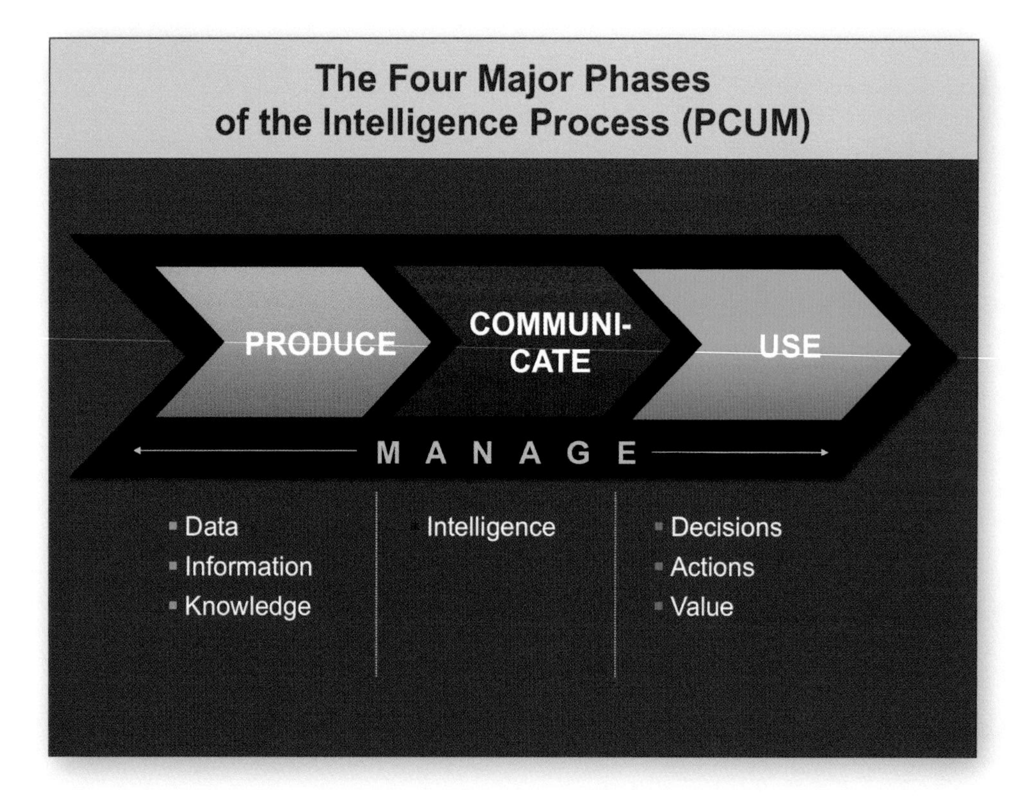

We're going to start at the 50,000-foot level, then zoom into each part of the KVC for more details. At this top level, there are four major process elements: Production, Communication, Use, and Management.

Knowledge production is what intelligence professionals and other knowledge workers do. Knowledge professionals are tasked with acquiring knowledge, but are not typically empowered to apply it.

Knowledge use consists of applying that knowledge. In a large organization, production and use are split, and the *decision maker* is the one empowered to act. In public affairs a decision maker is called a *policy maker,* but the role is fundamentally similar.

Because there are different roles (and different people) involved in producing versus using knowledge, there is a hand-off at some point—we call this ***communication***.

Finally, there is a ***management*** layer outside the whole chain. Management supports and integrates the other parts of the process. This includes the oversight of each step and phase of the process, the relationships between the steps and phases, and the relationships with other business processes.

Some refer to this as *knowledge management.* We prefer the term *intelligence management,* because it highlights the critical role that intelligence plays in bridging production and use.

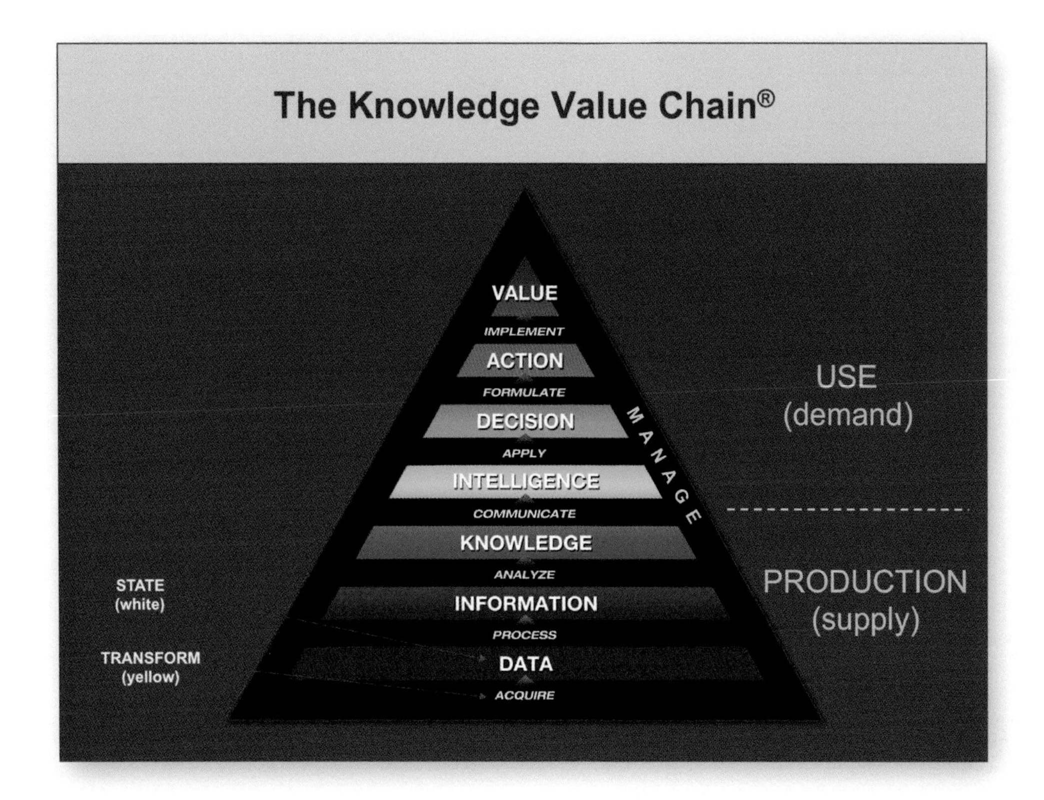

Now we're going to zoom down to 5,000 feet to see more detail. At each step there is a ***state*** (or stage of processing)—these are the colored bars with white lettering. There is also a ***transform*** (an action or series of action steps) needed to move from one state to the next—these are the words on the black bars in yellow.

There are seven KVC steps, each consisting of one transform that leads to one state. As in a manufacturing process, the output or product of one step becomes the input of the next.

This is similar to the input-output models of traditional economics. We have a *supply side* called ***Production***, and a *demand side* called ***Use***.

We call this the *Knowledge Value Chain®*. We could have just as effectively called it the "intelligence value chain," or even the "information value chain." Some people informally call it the "pyramid," some the "triangle."

The KVC is proprietary to TKA. There may be imitators—but this is the first and only true Knowledge Value Chain model!

KVC Analogies

KVC STATE	ALSO KNOWN AS
DATA	"Facts and figures"
INFORMATION	Trend lines; time series
KNOWLEDGE	Context; analysis
INTELLIGENCE	= Knowledge + Power
DECISION	= Intelligence + Group Process
ACTION	= Decision + Execution
VALUE	Results; outcomes

Knowledge professionals will recognize the ***state*** terms in the KVC model. For newcomers to the field and non-professionals (for whom the model can be equally useful) here are some synonyms and analogies.

Note that in this and the following two slides we're reading from the bottom up (whereas the KVC triangle reads from the top down.)

This slide shows the steps in abstract; the next slides shows how they might be applied in a strategic business situation, such as an acquisition.

Data are facts and figures—points of measurement. For example, the closing stock price of a company that might be an acquisition target is a data point.

When we process data it becomes ***Information***—for example, trend lines that represent the trends in stock price and trading volume over the past three years.

When we analyze the information, we create ***Knowledge***. We do this by adding context and meaning to the information. For example, we could look at a stock price, compared it to the overall market, compare it to comparable companies, and correlate it with actions the company has taken (such as announcing a new product.)

Knowledge is the highest level the typical knowledge professional can achieve acting alone. From there the knowledge must be communicated to an executive or decision maker, where it takes the form of ***Intelligence***.

>>

KVC Example—
A Business Acquisition

KVC STATE	EXAMPLE
DATA	Stock price of potential acquisition target
INFORMATION	Stock price; volume; market trends; "comparables" performance for prior three years
KNOWLEDGE	Stock price correlations with (1) company actions, (2) market as a whole, and (3) performance of similar companies
INTELLIGENCE	Review by senior business development executive
DECISION	Tender offer for public shares by management group
ACTION	Solicitation and execution of tender offer
VALUE	Acquisition of controlling shares

>>

The decision maker is the person empowered to act on the knowledge. In our example, an executive in charge of business development or acquisitions might review the data.

When an empowered individual has access to, and comprehension of, knowledge, it becomes intelligence. In short, "Knowledge + Power = Intelligence."

From there the decision maker typically takes control of the process. Typically, a ***Decision*** of any consequence is made in by a group, and there is a *group process* that comes into play. This involves consensus-building and sometimes actual voting. One decision maker might champion an idea, another might play devil's advocate, and a third might squarely oppose it. The process of discussion and debate can open up new possibilities and options.

In this example, management decides to tender an offer for a target's stock. When decisions are executed we have some kind of ***Action***—in this example, financing, executing, and publicizing the offer.

If the tender offer is successful, there is finally a business result—***Value*** is produced based on achieving our desired outcome. Significant value can be created by using intelligence as the foundation.

KVC Example—
Preempting a Competitive Offering

KVC STATE	EXAMPLE MERCK
DATA	Competitor files patent in key competitive technology space
INFORMATION	Compare with own product in that technology
KNOWLEDGE	Model competitor's product and conduct dummy market test
INTELLIGENCE	Present pro-forma financial results under both "do nothing" and "preempt" scenarios
DECISION	Attempt to preempt competitive space
ACTION	Reposition own existing product to counter competitor's presumed selling proposition
VALUE	Competitor reconsiders entry; product delayed 18-24 months; $150-200 million boost to Merck's top line

SOURCE: Clifford Kalb, *Competitive Intelligence Magazine* Jan-Feb 2002

SCIP Fellow Clifford Kalb provides a story that clearly illustrates the business value created by intelligence. Kalb ran a large intelligence team at Merck, the pharmaceutical company.

Merck intelligence, among other things, routinely mined public patent filings to identify developments of interest in the diagnostic categories in which they competed. One day they discovered that a rival was planning to enter a new category with a drug that was chemically similar to a drug that Merck already had on the market, but in a different category. Merck's intelligence team attended medical conferences and reviewed other public data to gain some understanding of how the rival drug was intended to be positioned in the marketplace.

Merck concluded that, by repositioning their own similar drug in the market space that the rival was planning to enter unchallenged, Merck could cause them to hesitate in their planned entry. In other words, they could preempt the rival entry.

This was neither a cost-free, nor a risk-free, move. Repositioning Merck's existing product would require significant outlays for communications and other forms of marketing.

The Merck team designed dummy market tests to model what was likely to happen if they executed the repositioning. They developed financial projections under each strategic scenario: "preempt" and "do nothing."

Kalb's team presented these fact-based projections to Merck's management team. Management bought into the preempt strategy, and committed the resources necessary to execute it.

The strategy worked—the rival's entry was delayed by an estimated 18-24 months. During that time Merck enjoyed unrivaled sales in that category—an incremental top-line value estimated at $150-200 million.

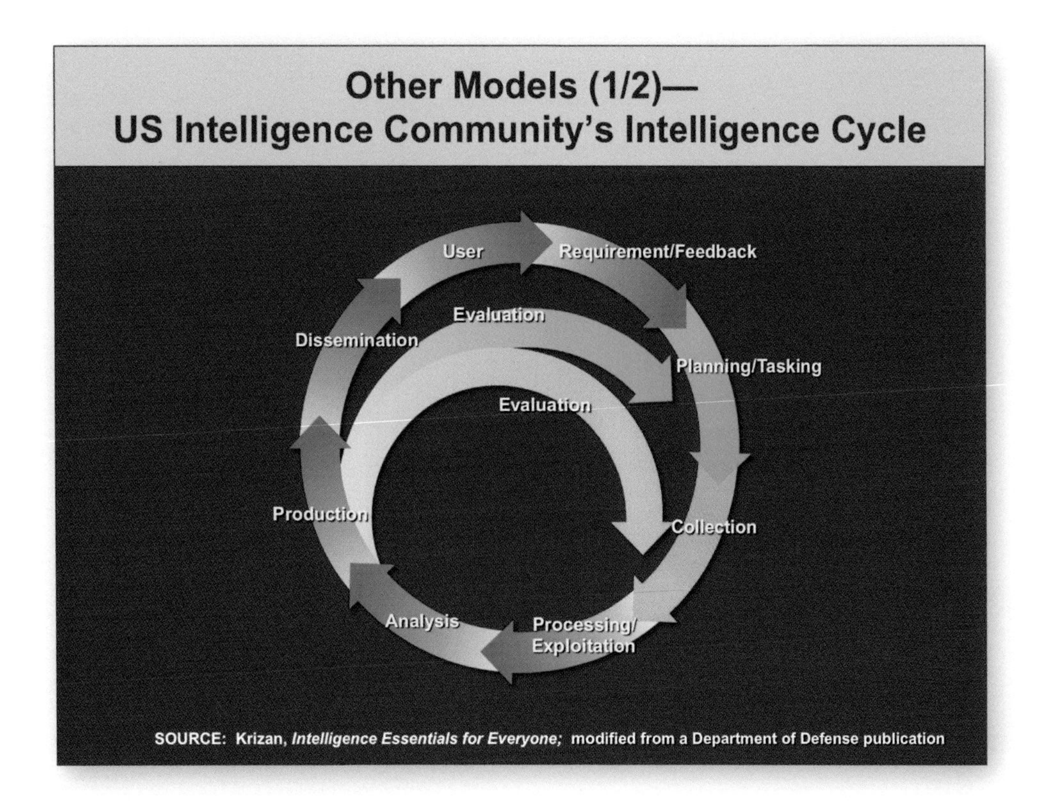

Intelligence scholar John Prescott notes that there are similarities between the KVC and the US government intelligence community's *intelligence cycle* ("i-cycle") model. This is natural, since they are alternative ways of describing similar phenomena.

However, there are signs that the i-cycle works less effectively than it once did. Of the many available critiques of the intelligence community's recent performance, some point to the i-cycle as part of the problem. One recent book by former intelligence officers remarks that, "A traditional bureaucratic model like the intelligence cycle is ill-suited for today's world, where intelligence users are highly varied and want tailored products, and where conditions are often changing." (*Best Truth*, Berkowitz and Goodman).

The i-cycle's applicability in corporate intelligence may be even more limited, for several reasons:

- **The i-cycle does not explicitly consider the value or benefit generated.** Public-sector intelligence is (rightly) regarded as a public good. As a result, it seems impervious to serious measurements of ROI. Intelligence rarely gets this same free pass in the business world.
- **The i-cycle only indirectly mentions the intelligence user.** Government intelligence intentionally separates the intelligence process from the decision-making process (*policy making*). This is done to preserve the independence of the two, which seems less of a concern in business.
- **The i-cycle seems like a static treadmill**—concerned with turning the crank, day after day. The highly customized and dynamic nature of typical business requirements is not reflected.

We caution businesses against uncritically adopting the i-cycle model, especially given that the government intelligence community itself has started searching for alternatives.

Until now, there has been no intelligence model "of business, by business, and for business." We propose the KVC as a step in this direction. The KVC is designed for organizations with finite resources that seek a positive ROI on intelligence—as they do for every business process.

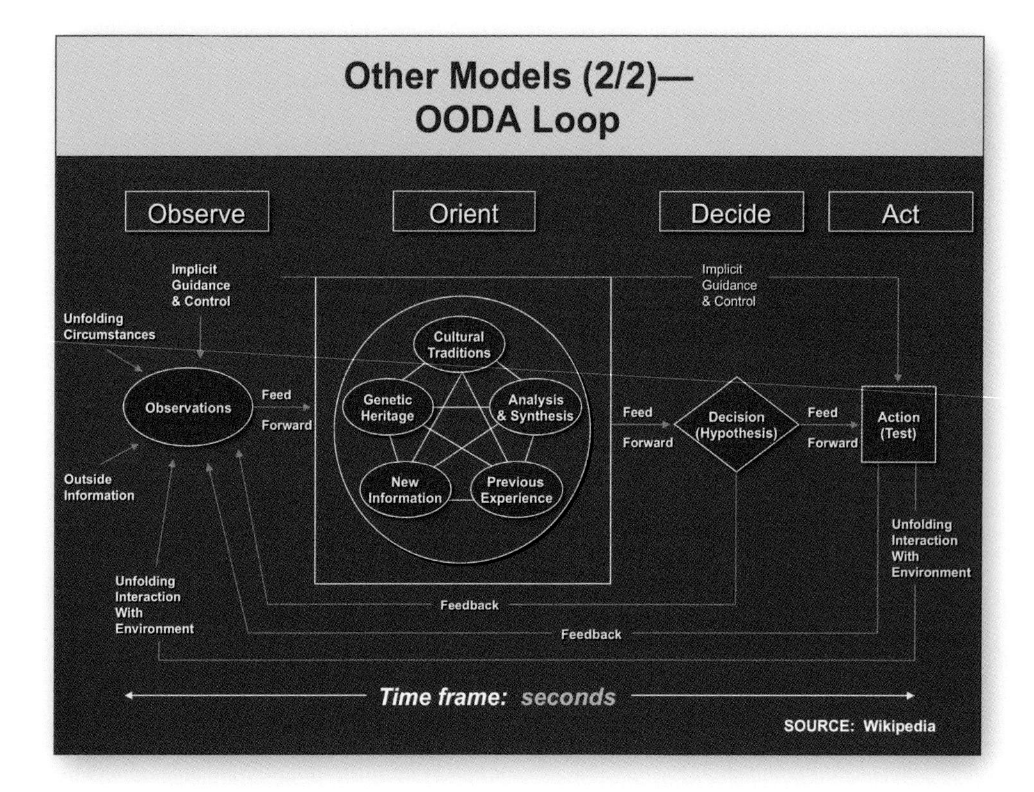

There are other models that resemble some elements of the KVC. One is called the *OODA loop* for its key elements—Observe, Orient, Decide, Act. Developed by military strategist John Boyd, this model is used in training fighter jet pilots.

The use of OODA loops in pilot training underscores the fact that the model can be made to operate in a compressed time frame—even one a few seconds long.

With training and practice, the KVC can become second nature, such that it is no longer a conscious, deliberate process. It becomes intuitive and embedded into the analyst's practice and ways of thinking.

OODA loops have elements in common with the *adaptive loops* developed by organizational learning theorists (Sense-Interpret-Decide-Act). (See *Adaptive Enterprise* by Stephan Haeckel.)

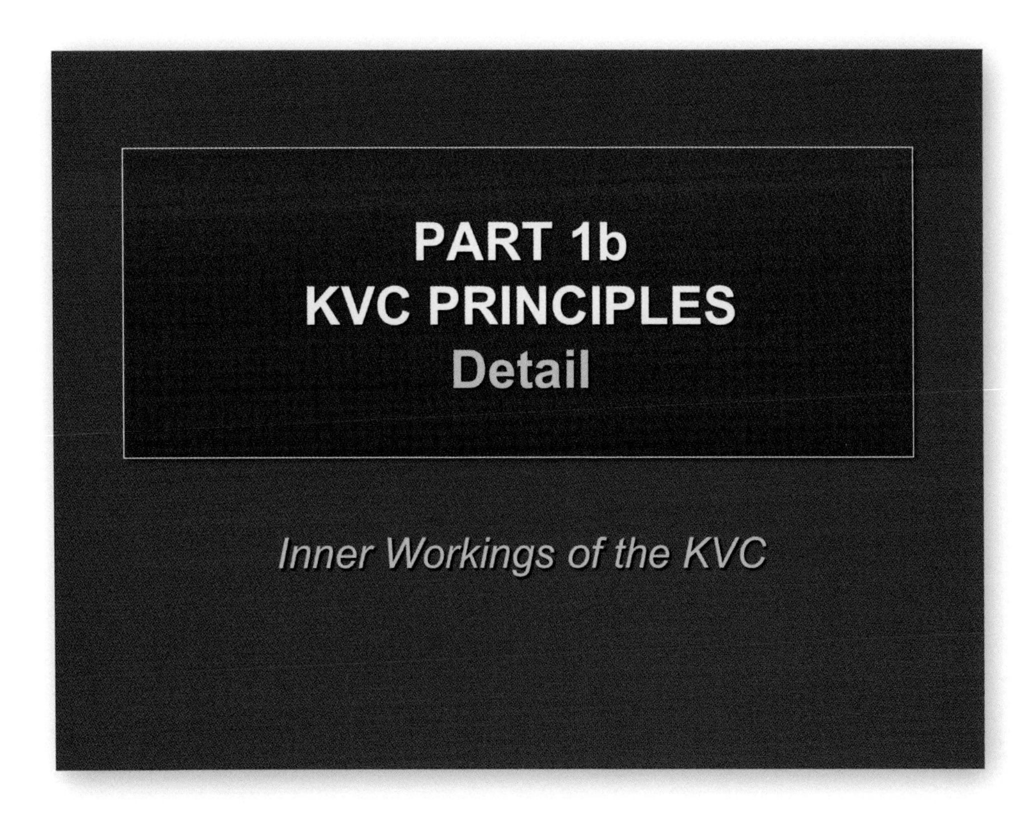

Here we'll present more detail about each step in the KVC. The inputs, actions, and outputs of each step are described, along with supporting resources at each step. This section is our cookbook and contains one big recipe—for turning data into value.

As you read this section, begin to think about the extent to which your intelligence projects, products, and processes meet these criteria.

In the *Appendix* (starting p. 89), we'll give you even more specific guidance on how to troubleshoot your intelligence process.

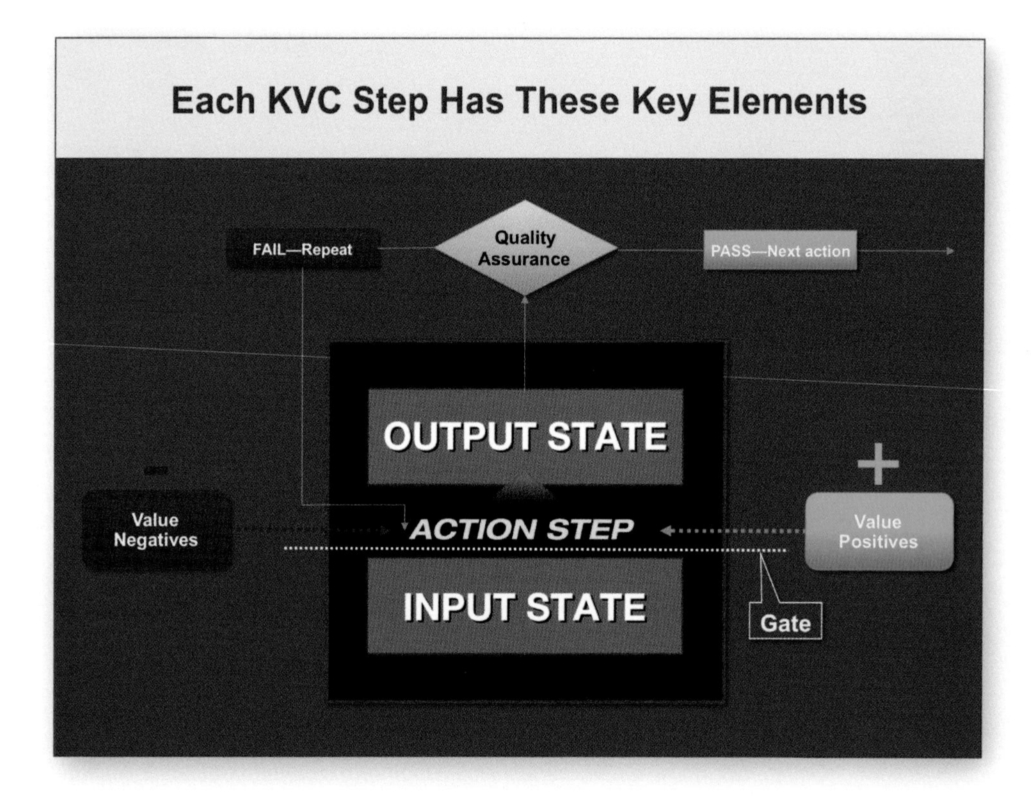

Now we're descending to 500 feet, to see the detail of each step of the KVC. These steps can help you (1) diagnose the problem or problems you are having in your KVC and (2) formulate actions to correct them.

All KVC steps have certain elements in common. Each step has an ***input state*** (the result of the previous step) and an ***output state***. Each step has a *transform* or ***action step*** that completes that transformation. Each action adds *cost* and adds *value*. (More of the latter than the former, ideally.) Each step also adds *time* to the overall KVC process.

At each step, there is a test both before and after the action is conducted. The pre-action test is called a ***gate***, and answers the question, "Is the next step worth taking?" A "no" answer here typically means the process is suspended.

The post-action test is ***quality assurance***, and answers the question, "Is the output of sufficient quality and completeness to move to the next step?" If the answer here is "no," then you need to correct (or even redo) the step. If the quality answer is "yes," you then need to ask the "gate" question for the subsequent step before proceeding.

The value added at each step is determined by the balance of ***value positives*** (which enhance value) and the ***value negatives*** (which fail to add, or can even erode, value.) For each step, you can increase the overall value added by specifically amplifying the value positives and by dampening or eliminating the value negatives.

Each Action Runs a Risk of "Breaking" the Value Chain!

KEY ISSUES

- Has the gate value been reached?
- How much cost has been added?
- How much value has been added?
- Is the quality of the output up to our specifications?
- Is it worth the additional investment to execute the next action?

There are seven sequential KVC steps, plus a pre-step for the whole cycle (Planning) and a post-step (Feedback). Factoring in the Management overlay, there are a total of *ten major opportunities to produce or destroy value*.

To make things even more challenging, the process is *serial* and errors are *cumulative*. An error at any given step tends to perpetuate itself throughout the chain. For example, if you do good analysis on faulty data, or on the wrong data, there is a good chance your conclusions will be wrong. "Garbage in, garbage out."

Likewise, you can capture great data and conduct great analysis on the *wrong* value drivers or issues. This is one of the most common shortcomings in intelligence, and is rarely within the direct control of the intelligence producer.

Sir Colin McColl of the British intelligence agency MI6 once said, of military intelligence, "Finding the right answers is relative easy. The hard part is asking the right questions." It's true in business too.

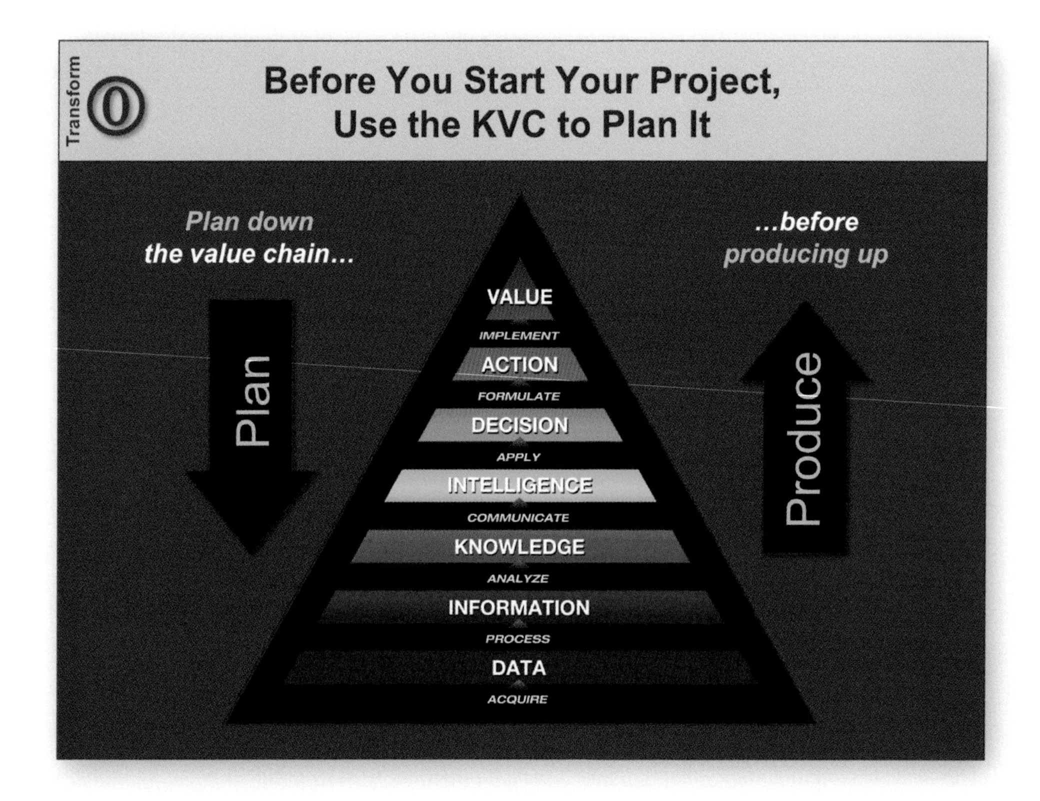

In executing an intelligence initiative, do not start at the bottom of the pyramid—start at the top. Even before Transform 1 of the KVC (acquiring data), there is a "Transform 0"—***Planning*** the project. For recurring efforts, this can be done once, with periodic adjustments as needed. For one-shot projects, it needs to be done each time.

In Planning, the producer and user develop a *shared understanding* of basic project parameters—the time frame required, the budget, the project outputs or deliverables, the interim milestones and communications to be provided, the organization of the project team, and so on.

What use will be made of the information? Is it need-to-know, mission-critical information? Or is it merely nice-to-know? What is the effort's proposed *value payout?* What is at stake?

Most intelligence producers have been trained to ask these questions. However intelligence clients may give incomplete answers, either because they don't know (if they are intermediaries), or because of security restrictions. "Get me everything on..." is the way many unsuccessful efforts start.

When possible, develop these understandings in a direct interaction with the user—phone or face-to-face meetings are best, but email can work, too. One of the parties should then commit the project plan to a written document, in at least outline format. This can be reviewed up-front for mutual understanding on all of the items, used during the project as a "punch list" of steps that must be completed, and may play a key role in quality assurance at the end of the effort.

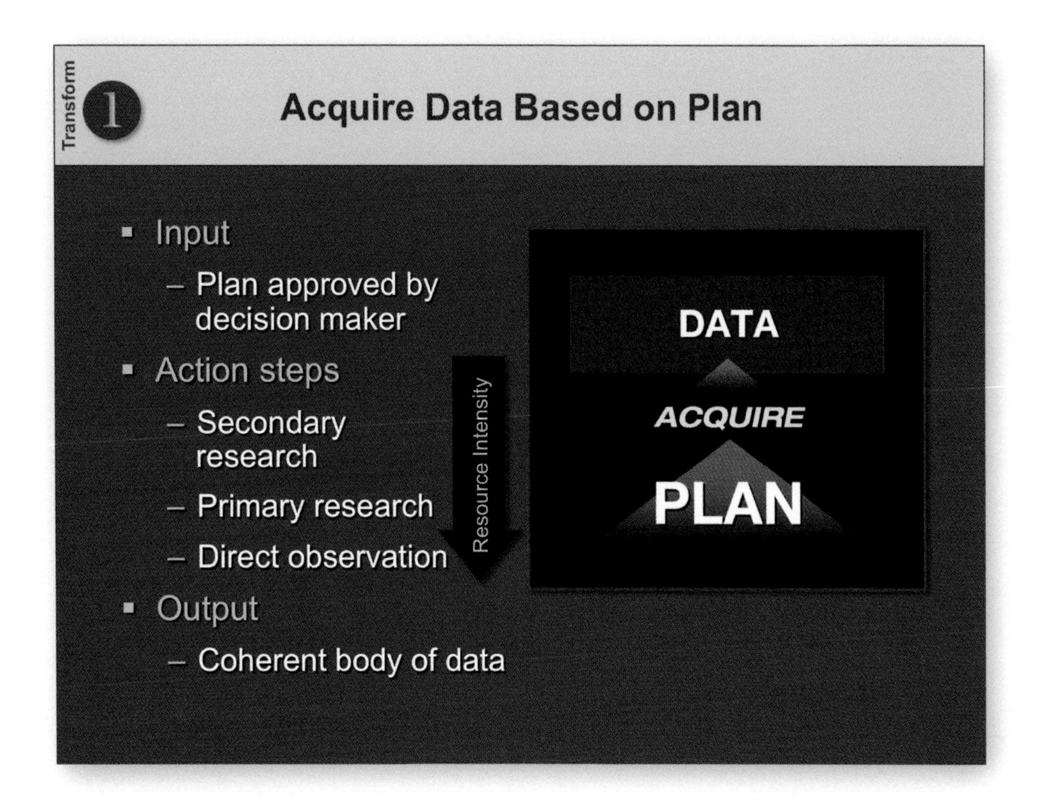

Data acquisition is the subject of hundreds of books and articles, and an in-depth treatment is outside our scope here. We call it "data acquisition" (rather than "data collection") to highlight that there is always a resource cost—either an actual financial expenditure or an expenditure of time and effort on someone's part.

The sources and techniques for gathering data evolve continually. There are three fundamental types of data acquisition—secondary research, primary research, and direct observation.

In ***secondary research***, you read what someone has written about a topic of interest. Because it is often faster, less expensive, and (thanks to the Internet) more widely available than primary research, secondary research is usually undertaken first in the knowledge acquisition process. (The terminology refers to the proximity to knowledge, not the order of the process.)

However, secondary research is, by definition, less tailored to a particular goal than primary, and there is typically no interaction with the source of the information. Secondary sources are subject to the reportorial and editorial biases of the source, and to the filtering-out process that such a source invariably introduces.

In ***primary research***, you dialogue with someone in real-time about a topic of interest about which they have first-hand knowledge. This knowledge can be a *fact* (for example, a private company's annual sales) or an *opinion* (for example, what trends are affecting a particular industry). The interaction can take place in person, by phone, or by email.

In ***direct observation*** you acquire direct, first-hand knowledge of the subject. This is sometimes overlooked as a source, though it can be quite powerful. The Internet blurs distinctions here. For example, I've looked at a Google Earth photo of a building to estimate its capacity. While not the same as observing it in person, it's nearly as effective—and a lot less costly.

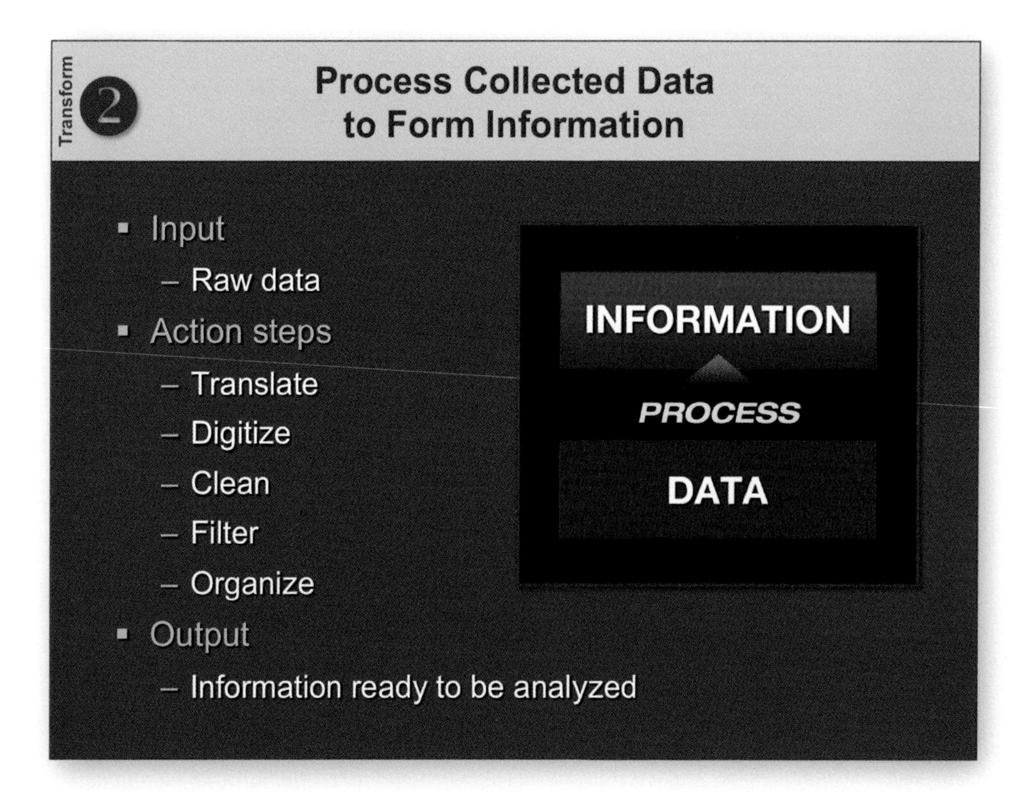

Processing is the most misunderstood—and most frequently neglected—step in the KVC. Before you start analyzing, there is an essential intermediate step of 'cleaning' the data, or otherwise preparing it for analysis.

For example, you might need to translate content from one language into the language the analyst speaks.

Some change of format may be needed. For example, you may need to transcribe interview notes, or enter the data into a spreadsheet or some other easily manipulated electronic format.

You need to look at the data to identify any *outliers*—observations so far removed from the trend that they are most likely in error. These should be either corrected or eliminated before the analysis.

Although "outliers" typically refers to quantitative data (numbers), this same step applies equally to qualitative data (text and ideas). For example, in conducting an interview, you may need to discount some of the things that someone says, depending on his credibility and past history of reliability. Few sources have complete and unlimited credibility. Just because someone says that something is true does not necessarily mean that it is.

Organizing the data into categories for analysis can be a great time saver and will improve the quality of the analysis.

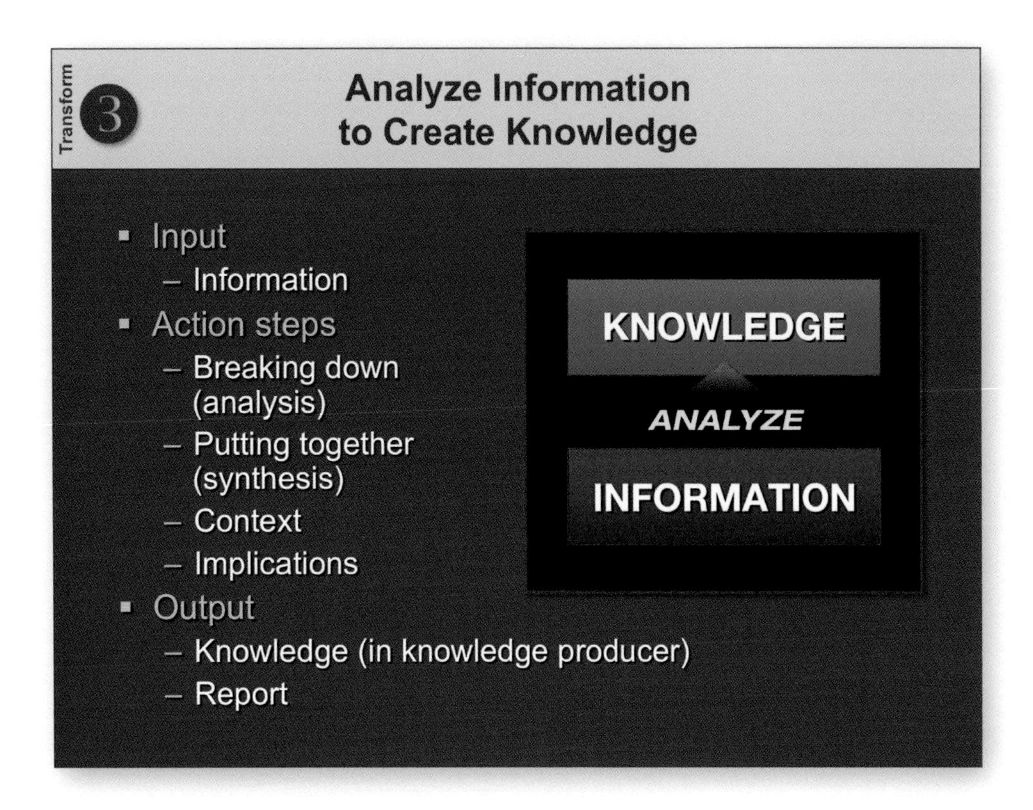

Once your data set is clean and organized, you're ready to ***analyze*** the information. There many types of business analysis that may be useful in a given business situation. Some of these are productized, and even commoditized. To see examples, look at your favorite financial source—mine are Yahoo! and Barron's—to see P/E ratios, stock trends, and other basic kinds of financial analysis.

What you're typically doing is *analyzing* (i.e., breaking things down), then *synthesizing* (i.e., putting them back together) in a way that is most relevant to your business problem.

Often the best analysis is the one created specifically for the situation at hand. But if you're not feeling creative, there are strategy books that can teach you the tried-and-true approaches.

Analysis—like the rest of the KVC—needs to be responsive to the value payout at the top of the pyramid. Assume, for example, that your strategy is to buy market share in a given segment by cutting your prices below those of your rivals. In that case, you'd want to analyze their prices and margins over time, as well as look at the market share assumptions that could result from changing your price relative to theirs.

Don't forget to factor in a likely retaliation on their part. They will probably not let their prices be undercut; they may cut prices to match, or even go below, your prices. Failing to factor potential competitive response into a strategic analysis is a common mistake, and often a costly one.

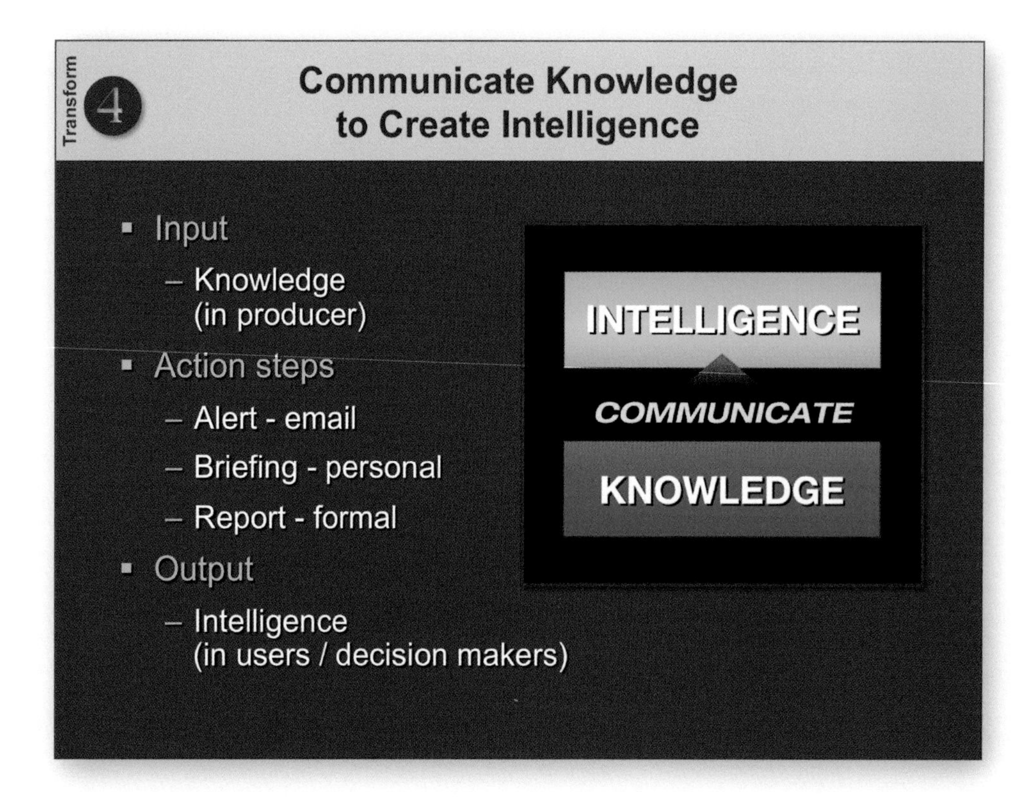

Now the intelligence producer has some knowledge to ***communicate*** to the user/decision maker/client. Our research shows that communication is the action step most fraught with problems. This is partly because there is often a culture gap between "knowledge people" (intelligence producers) and "power people" (intelligence users). Working together, producers and users can create powerful synergies, but the relationship is often complex and problematic.

Producers and users typically represent different "tribes" of the organization's culture. Producers tend to have training in intelligence, library science, or information technology—and less experience in the business than their clients. Users tend to have MBAs, law degrees, and/or significant operating experience. Producers tend to be younger and less formal; users, older and more formal. Pay scales and career paths are typically different.

This *knowledge-value gap* creates barriers to effective trust-building and communication. One of these is the issue of *gate value*. How do you determine whether a piece of intelligence is important enough to be communicated to a decision maker—or whether it will just be a distraction for that person? If she has asked for the intelligence, the answer is clear—you must pass it along.

However, a producer achieves a much greater ability to add value once he becomes *anticipatory*—able to communicate intelligence *that has not been explicitly requested*. Our research shows this is what most intelligence users want. But with that comes the responsibility of making independent judgments about what is *signal* necessary for the decision maker to know, and what is *noise* that actually gets in the way of her understanding the situation.

Inexperienced intelligence producers tend to deliver too much noise with the signal. Volume of output is far less important than its quality and relevance. Recall what happened to the shepherd boy in Aesop's fable "The Boy Who Cried Wolf."

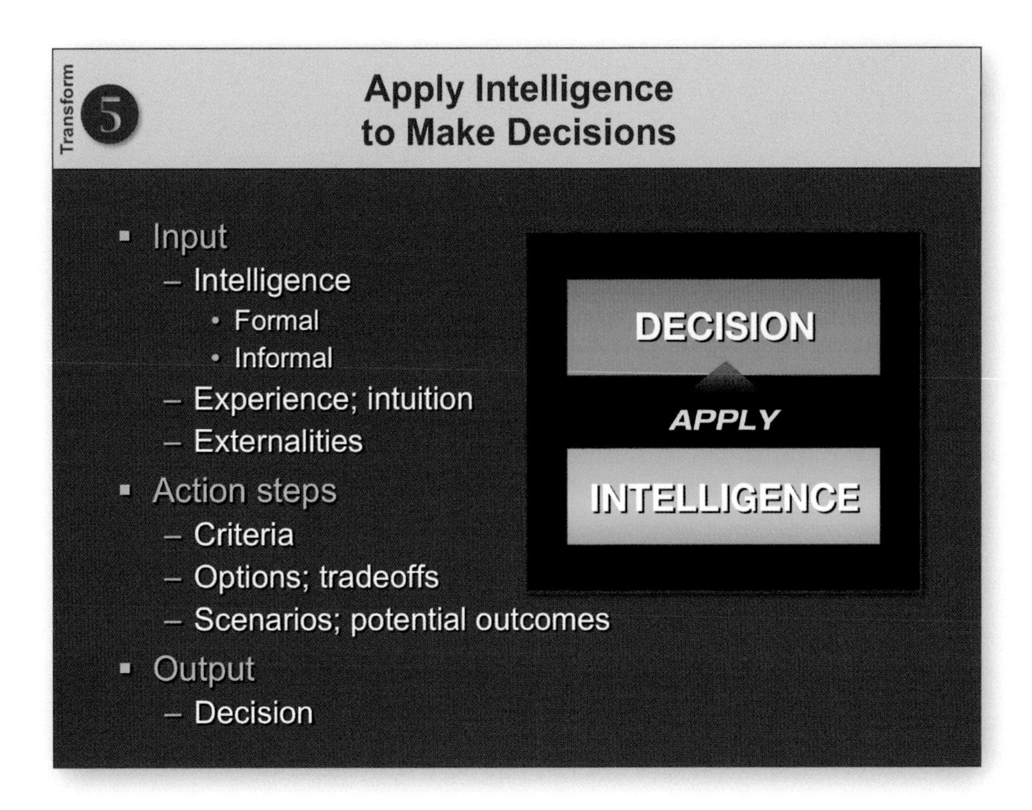

At the ***decision*** stage, primary responsibility shifts to the user(s). In the event a course correction is needed, there should always be a feedback loop to earlier steps.

Not only is *formal* intelligence (like the KVC) considered, there is also *informal* intelligence—a powerful force, since it usually comes from close and trusted sources. Sometimes a conversation with a trusted advisor runs counter to what the formal intelligence says. This "word-of-mouth" intelligence, which is typically anecdotal and not rigorous, should not be categorically ignored by the decision maker. Sometimes word-of-mouth can be the source of *weak signals* that travel faster through social networks than through formal intelligence channels, thus enabling early warning. On the other hand, informal intelligence is often weighted more heavily by the user than is warranted, and checked less carefully, due to the familiarity and "trustedness" of its source.

Decision makers are hired, not because they are decision-making robots, but because they have a wealth of experience, contacts, and intuition that have led them to be successful in the past. These resources should augment and amplify—but not replace—more rigorous intelligence.

Finally, there are *externalities* that come into play in making decisions, especially ones in groups. There may be political favors to repay. There may be coalitions that line up against each other. The criteria upon which a decision should ideally be made may be unclear or not agreed upon.

It's often difficult to know when a decision should be—or must be—made. This is not something taught well in business schools. There, you know when your decision is needed—when the class discussion starts! In the real world, how do you know when a decision is needed? Decision making is part science and part art, and the timing of decisions is within the 'art' part.

You *apply* intelligence to make a decision. Can you make a decision without using intelligence? Yes, just flip a coin. There's a 50% chance you'll be right—is that good enough?

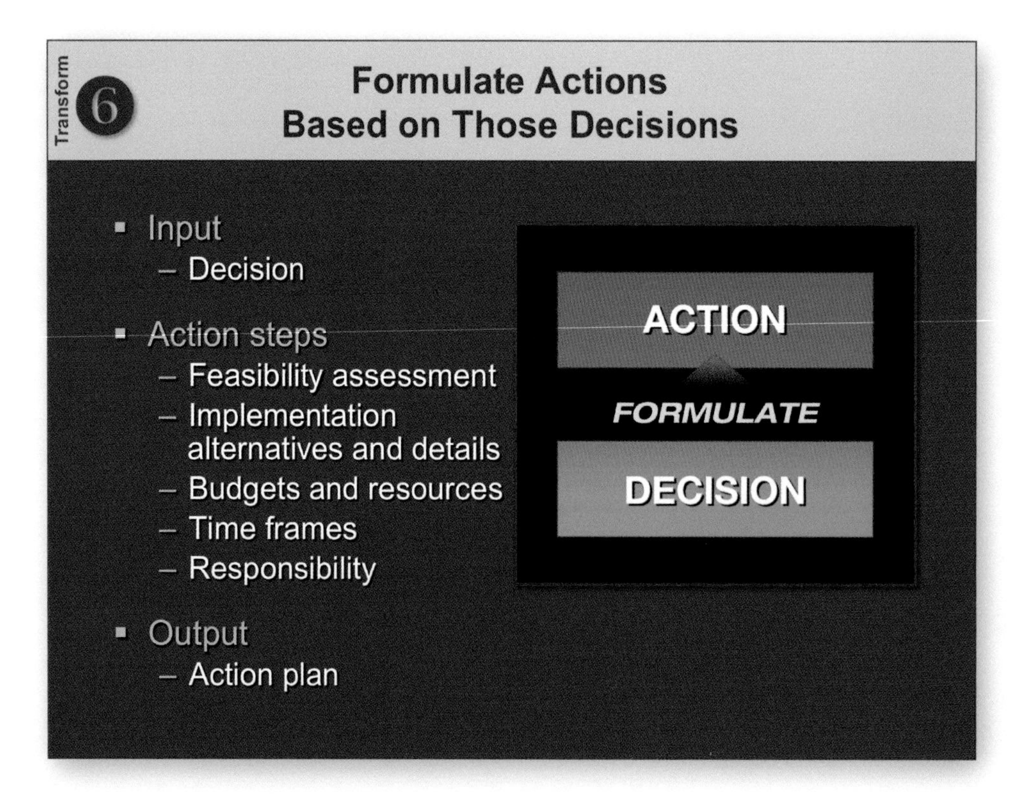

Even though they're called decision makers, they are not producing value unless—and until—some ***actions*** are taken that execute those decisions. Actions themselves must be thought through and require significant planning of details.

For example, their feasibility needs to be assessed; alternatives for implementation should be discussed; budgets need to be created, and resources allocated; time frames and milestones need to be specified; and responsibilities and accountability need to be assigned.

Decision makers are also called *executives*—literally, people who execute and get things done. This reflects the action-taking nature of their role.

CASE EXAMPLE

I once worked in a state agency tasked with implementing a new and complex federal law. The law as passed by Congress was only the beginning. Standing between the law (which was, in effect, a cluster of related policy decisions) and its implementation (which was our responsibility at the state level) was a federal agency responsible for administering that law.

Their job was to draft a set of regulations that spelled out the detailed actions, resources, and requirements needed in order to carry out the law consistently with the intent of Congress. They also served as technical support in clarifying and answering our questions about the law.

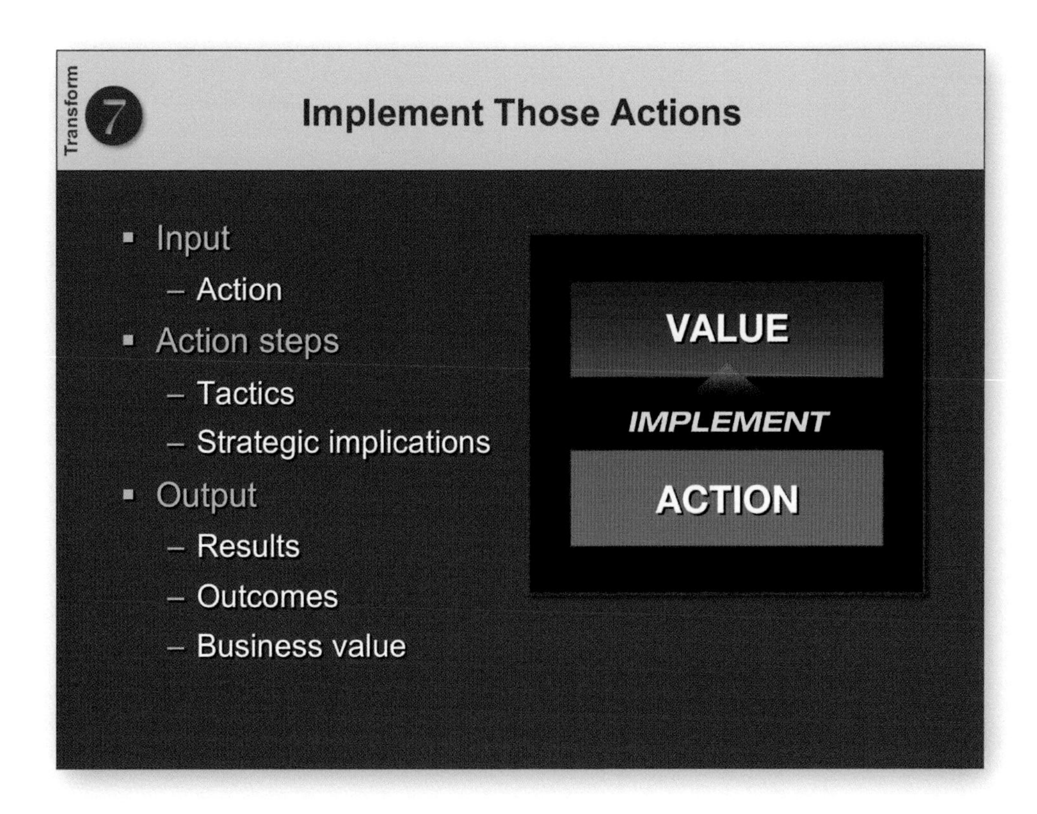

Everything up to now prepares us to finally produce value. *Implementation* or execution is the last step in the KVC before the top—and even here the chain can die.

Plans may go unimplemented for a number of reasons. A crisis might divert key resources and attention. A sudden change in business conditions might cause a last-minute hesitation for budgetary reasons. A key executive champion could leave the organization.

Or the implementation may proceed, but be executed poorly—using the wrong or insufficient resources, for example. There may be unforeseen impediments, obstacles, and slowdowns.

If little is done to implement the action plan, or if the implementation is for any reason insufficient or ineffective, little will change. Results will not be achieved, and value will not be produced.

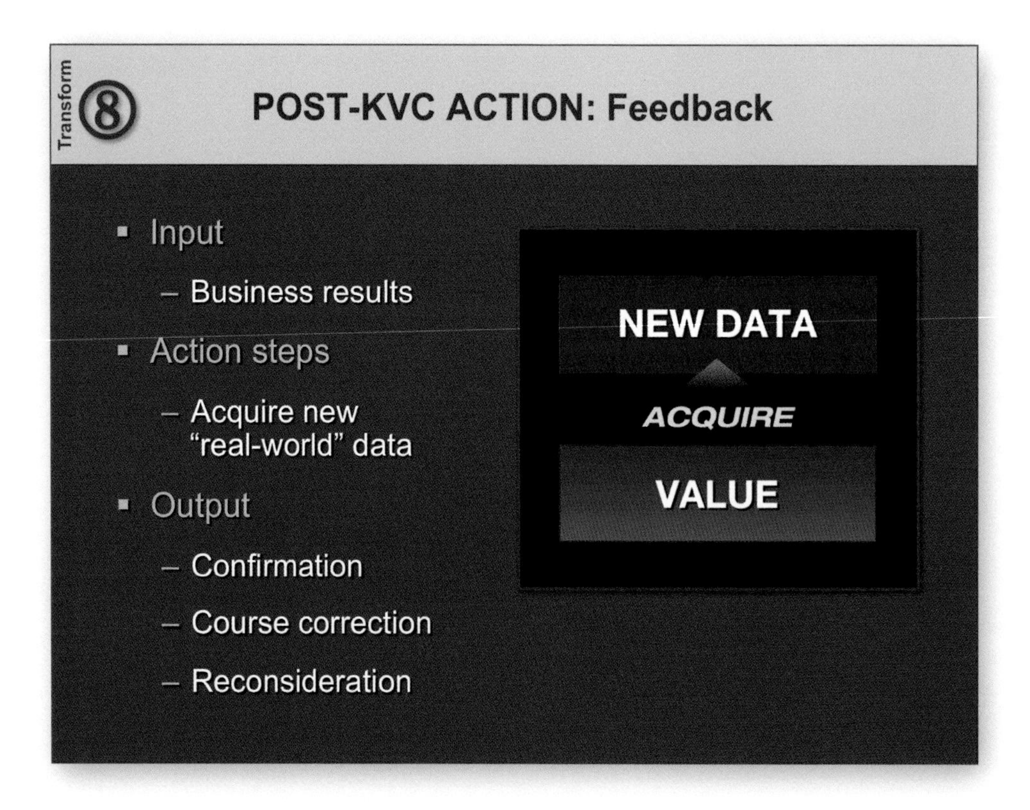

Let's assume that we proceed with implementation of our action plans, and that implementation succeeds as we planned. While we're in implementation mode, there is a ***feedback*** loop that enables us to acquire new data and make course corrections as needed. In fact, this is the most valuable data, because it is real-world feedback, and no longer just a research project.

When a consumer packaged goods company launches a new product—a major decision involving huge resources over a long period—they first collect large amounts of data to see if the product is feasible. But then, before launching the product nationally, they introduce the product in a small number of representative *test markets*. These tests are real in the sense that you can buy the real product. The manufacturer can test alternative scenarios for pricing, packaging, and promotion.

Market tests usually give a reliable indication of how well the product will sell in a wider launch—but at much less expense and risk than a full national rollout would require. This represents a high-ROI investment in market intelligence.

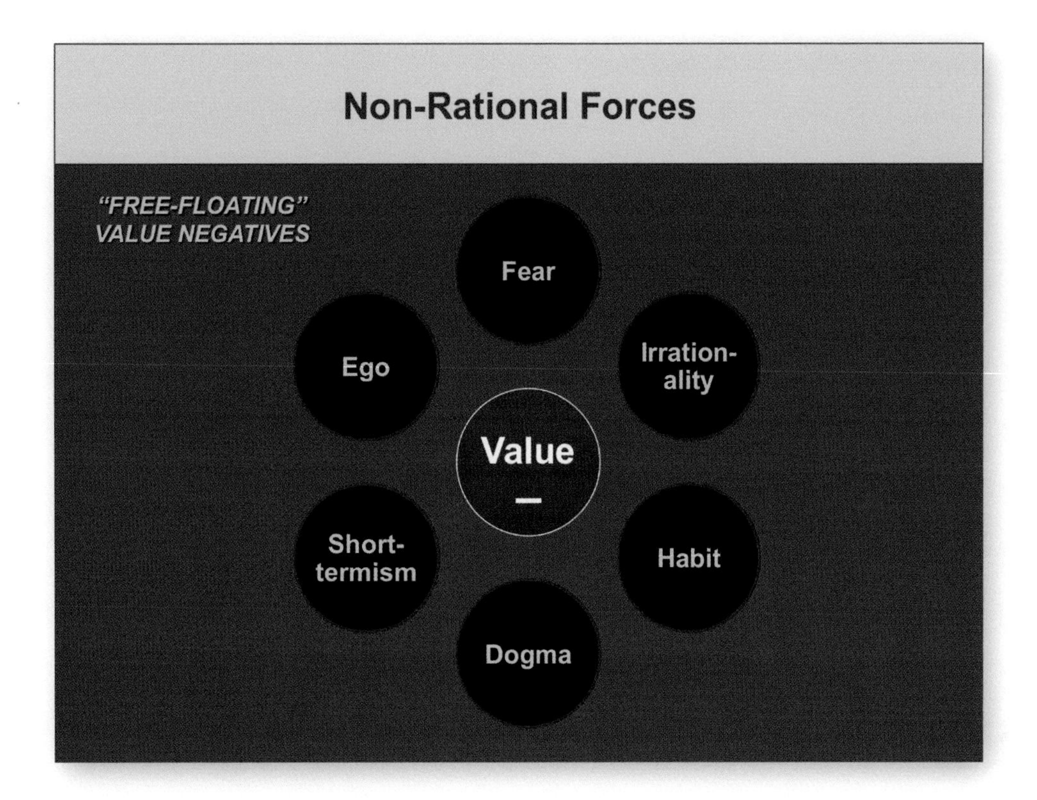

The Knowledge Value Chain is an organized, rational model of how decision making works at its best. Do things really work that way?

Not always. There are many forces that can work against the rational methods we have presented here. Some of the most important ones are listed in the slide. You will run into them continually, and you need to be aware they exist so you are not blind-sided.

It's best to think of the KVC model partly as "how things work" and partly as "how things *should* work in an optimized situation."

The field of behavioral economics has recently produced many books about the irrationality of human economic decision making. (See, for example, *Thinking, Fast and Slow* by Daniel Kahneman.) Making decisions in groups can be even more complex, because you have to balance the *wisdom of crowds* with the occasional *madness of crowds.*

In groups, extraneous factors that have little relevance to the content of the decision can influence that decision. The KVC addresses some of these insofar as they influence specific steps in the chain (see the *Scorecard* in the Appendix), but these free-floating negatives are best addressed by a wider organizational culture-change initiative.

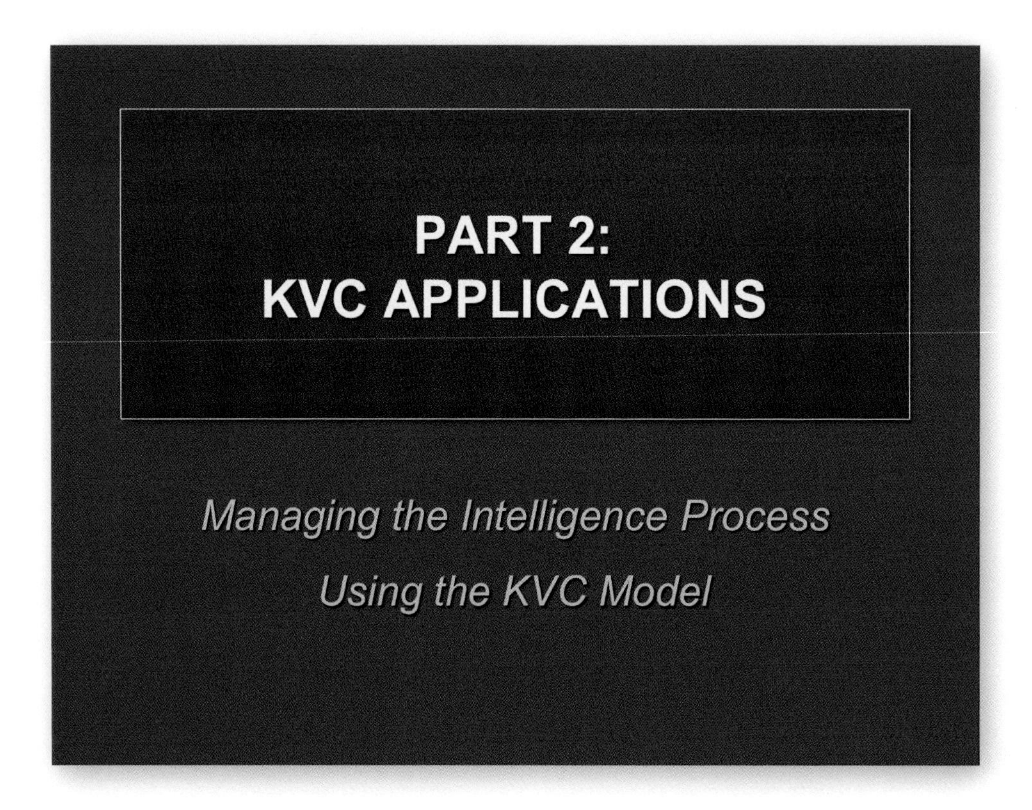

By now you have some knowledge of the KVC and how it works. But it hasn't yet produced value for you, because you have not yet used it to solve business problems.

In this section we'll see how the KVC can be applied to manage intelligence, and, in particular, to solve common intelligence problems.

Some of these come from the TKA casebook. Others come from clients who have contributed their observations. Others are ideas that we think have merit, but that are waiting to be tested by people like you.

Some of these are at the *project management* level (where we first developed the model). Others are at the *intelligence product* level—reports and briefings. Still others are at a more macro-enterprise *intelligence process* level.

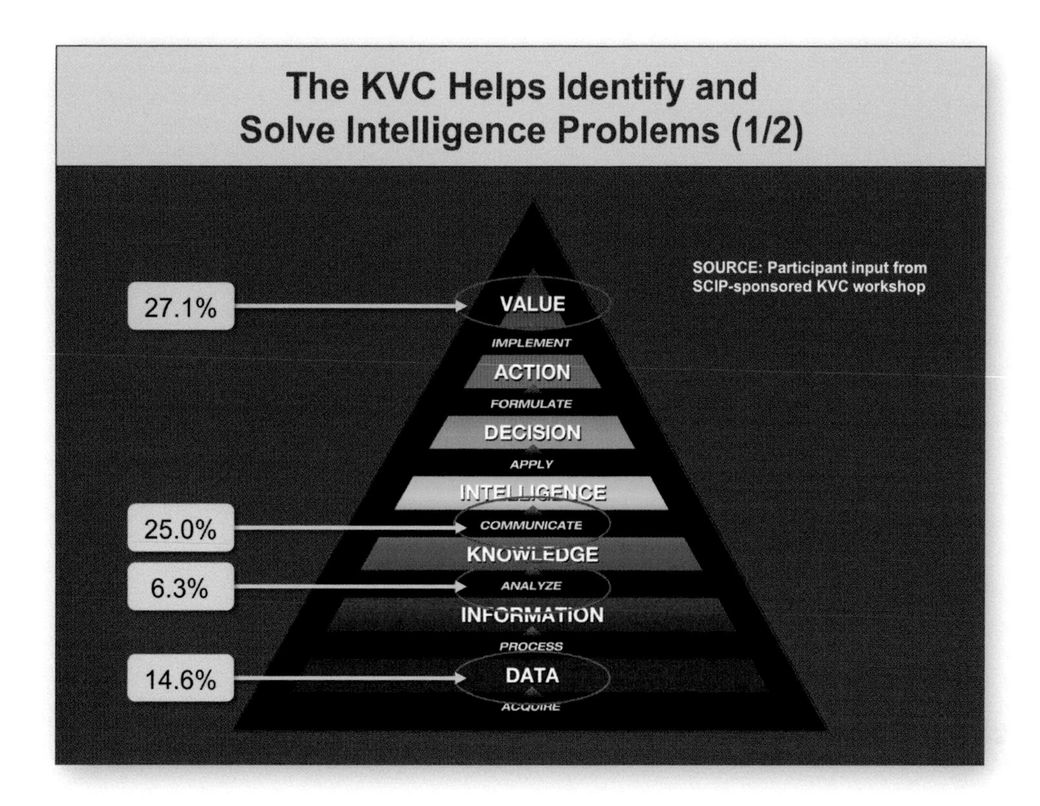

Each intelligence process or project has many chances to succeed—or fail. The KVC describes 10 major areas in which these occur. Certain areas consistently prove more problematic than others for many organizations. Mapping problematic areas against the KVC model can give you an initial idea of what might be wrong, and how to approach fixing it.

Results from an early public KVC workshop sponsored by the Society of Competitive Intelligence Professionals (SCIP) are shown above. Participants were asked to name their three most difficult intelligence challenges—their "Points of Pain." Their responses were then mapped into the steps (states and transforms) in the KVC. The result shows a distinct clustering where these trouble spots occurred most frequently.

In the early days of corporate intelligence, acquisition of data was one of the most frequently mentioned challenges. Here it was mentioned in almost 15% of the responses.

Challenges mentioned most frequently involved not being sure that intelligence is creating value—or, if it is, how it does so. The single most problematic action step was *communication*, the interface between the knowledge professional and the decision maker.

Upcoming sections offer ideas on how to address these common intelligence challenges.

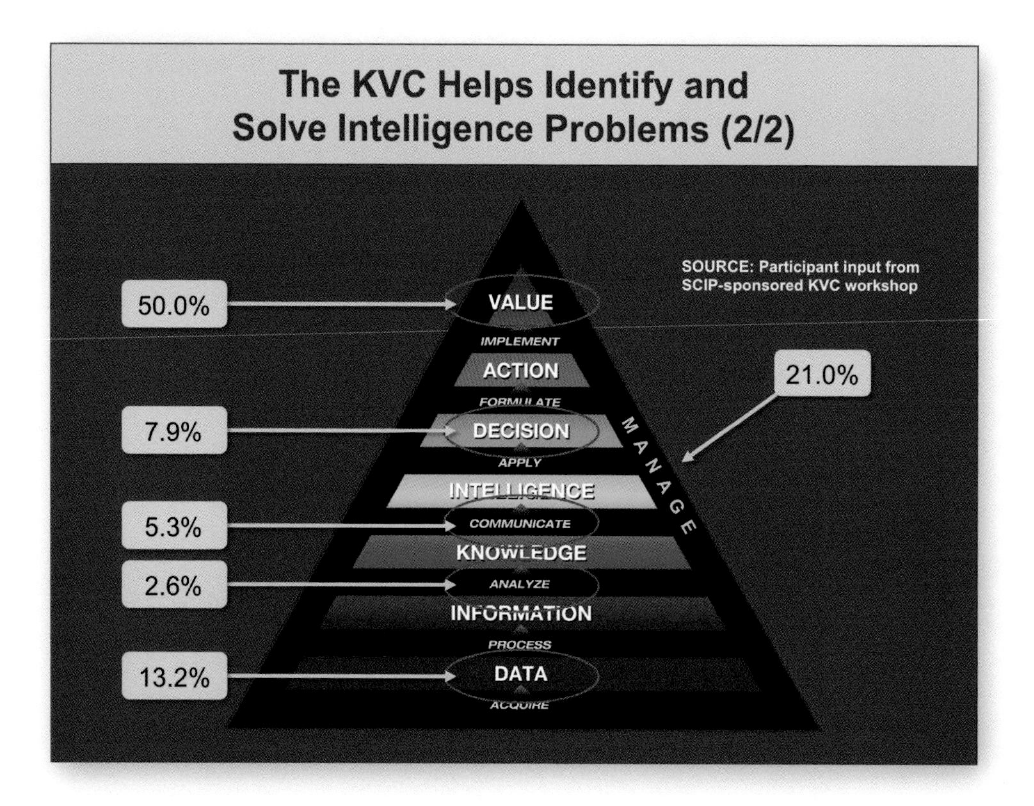

Results from a more recent KVC workshop are shown above. Compared with the previous slide, note that there is more concern at the top of the pyramid—especially in the *Value* segment, where half of the problems occur. Comments such as "I need more resources" and "I'm always being cut at budget time" indicate that value is not being created—at least not sufficiently, in the perception of managers (which is largely what counts.)

In this research, we found many responses that didn't fit neatly into the KVC categories. So we added a new KVC category: *management.* This turned out to be our second most-challenging area. Management issues affect all aspects of the KVC and include things such as:

- building the right structure for an intelligence unit;
- where the unit should be positioned within the organization;
- how to build an internal intelligence network; and
- how to gain the confidence and support of management.

Intelligence "Points of Pain" 1

- **SYMPTOM:**
  *"We don't know how…
  or even IF…
  intelligence creates value."*
- **KVC LOCATION:**
  Value
- **TYPICAL CAUSES:**
  - Insufficient understanding of client problem or situation
  - Lack of "client training"
- **POTENTIAL SOLUTIONS**
  - Be sure an adequate dialogue precedes project
  - Discuss how intelligence is expected to create value
  - Clearly define project parameters
  - Create conditions for an ongoing dialogue

I've worked with many intelligence practitioners in a range of organizations. It always amazes me how similar their problems are. The next few slides depict the more common of these Points of Pain.

In my experience, the most prevalent intelligence problem of all is knowing how—or even if—one is helping produce ***value***. Many intelligence consumers are relatively unsophisticated about the intelligence process, and are not readily able to discern good intelligence from bad. The test of user value usually comes in hindsight, when the producer's estimate is proven to have been either right or wrong.

A producer's insufficient understanding of his client's problem is a leading cause of this value misunderstanding.

Problems also arise when user expectations are set and/or managed ineffectively. Shared expectations between user and producer, updated when and if conditions change, are essential for optimal client relations and project outcomes.

The best way to assess the value that a piece of intelligence is expected to create is to discuss this frankly with the user, in advance of project execution. In this way, the magnitude and importance of the effort can be gauged.

The typical user seeks intelligence as a means to a *solution* to her business problem. The intelligence is, in her view, a component or *raw material* that helps create that solution.

Intelligence "Points of Pain" 2

- **SYMPTOM:**
  "We do great analysis… but management doesn't use it well."
- **KVC LOCATION:**
  Communication
- **TYPICAL CAUSES:**
  - Lack of trusting relationship with client
  - Mismatched perspectives
- **POTENTIAL SOLUTIONS**
  - Do some "market research" with decision makers
    - Determine their communications preferences
  - Follow up on projects
    - Determine what was most useful
    - Determine where improvement is needed
  - Assess "portfolio" of current intelligence products

Communication is also a common trouble spot. This may manifest itself as, "The users don't trust what we're saying." Such a lack of trust can be performance-based—for example, "You were wrong in the past, why should we believe you now?" More often, though, it is a cultural bias, the hidden message of which is, "We have MBAs and lots of experience. Why should we listen to junior people who surf the Internet all day?"

Intelligence communication with decision makers is often routinized. We report to the senior team on Friday of each week, we speak to the CEO at 10am each Tuesday—that kind of thing. The time frame for such communication may be highly compressed, so it's important to maximize the impact of what communication does occur.

The best communication is not just one-way but actively seeks feedback from the user. This is why we prefer that term, which is related to "community," over the term "dissemination." The latter connotes a unidirectional spray of information or data.

Prior to transmitting intelligence, it is essential to know how a particular client prefers to communicate. Some prefer a lengthy and detailed email. Others prefer a few bullet points, a telephone briefing, or a face-to-face meeting.

Within a reasonable time after transmitting the intelligence, there should be a dialogue about the usefulness of the intelligence and any other follow-up that may be needed. An overall assessment of intelligence products should also be conducted periodically.

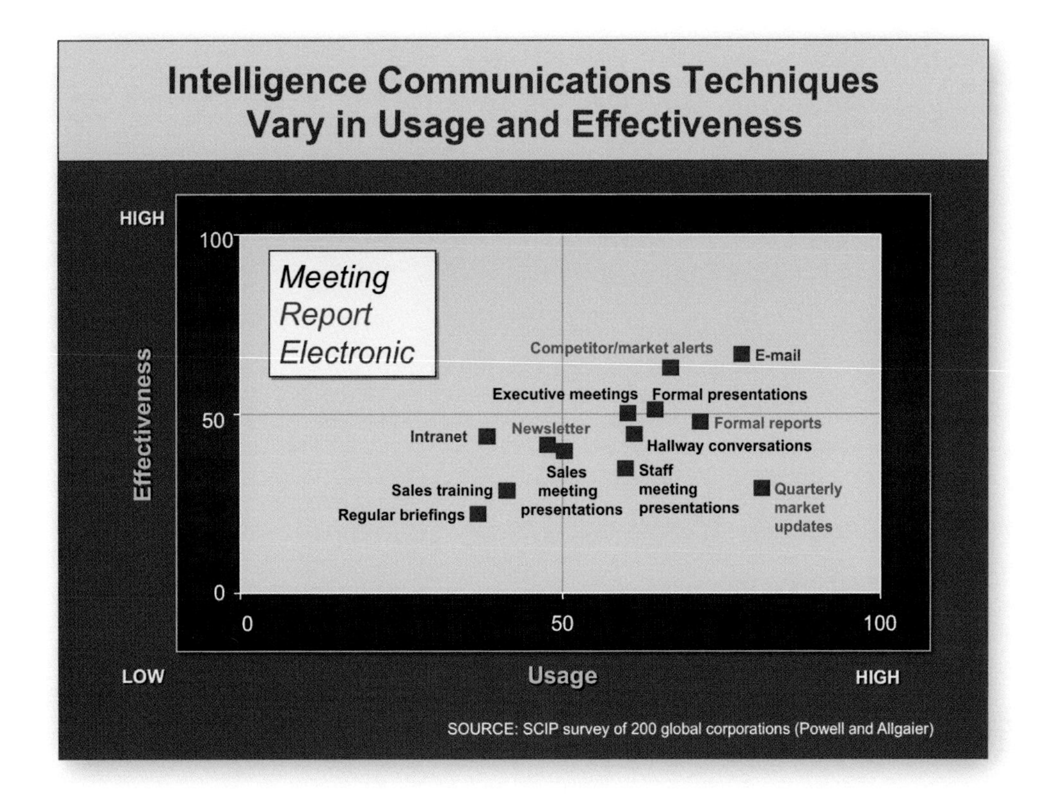

There are many communications techniques used for intelligence. These vary in effectiveness depending on factors like client preferences; the situation about which intelligence is needed; the speed of intelligence needed; and the number of clients involved.

The results shown here are from a benchmark study of more than 200 SCIP member companies designed and conducted by The Knowledge Agency in cooperation with SCIP Fellow Cyndi Allgaier. Each communications technique is color-coded by type: black for meetings; blue for hard-copy reports; and red for electronic.

Respondents rated each form of communication on its perceived level of ***usage*** in their organization and its level of ***effectiveness***. For the most part, we found a positive correlation between the levels of usage and effectiveness for a given technique. It's not clear which is cause and which is effect—is it used more because it's effective, or effective because it's used more often?

However, this positive correlation is not always the case. Some forms of communication may persist in spite of their limited perceived value. For example, we see that the quarterly market update, an often-used form of communication, is seen as relatively ineffective.

Any organization could implement a survey like this internally, and reduce or eliminate forms of communication that fall outside the desired usage-effectiveness ranges.

Intelligence "Points of Pain" 3

- **SYMPTOM:**
  "We have many KVCs... but they don't link with each other."
- **KVC LOCATION:**
  Management
- **TYPICAL CAUSE:**
  Organizational silos ("knowledge archipelago")
- **POTENTIAL SOLUTIONS**
  - Create a macro view of the major KVCs in your organization
    - Work group level
    - Enterprise level
  - Seek opportunities to redeploy information in value-enhancing ways

Any large, complex organization has thousands of KVCs. A KVC may be managed well on its own, but within a *silo*, or organizational niche, that inhibits its reuse outside that silo. Where many little islands of knowledge remain unconnected, we call this a "knowledge archipelago."

Sometimes this silo-ization is intentional, and is the result of organizational *turf conflict*. Such conflict can, in turn, can be brought on by budget issues. ("I bought it, therefore I won't share it with you.")

More often, though, it is unintentional, in that one silo may not be fully aware of what another is doing or is interested in.

One approach here is to first build a macro overview of the major KVCs in a work group or entire enterprise—then to seek out and develop opportunities for them to reuse some parts of their KVCs. A working session that integrates various organizational elements within a single company can be an excellent way to identify and begin solving these problems.

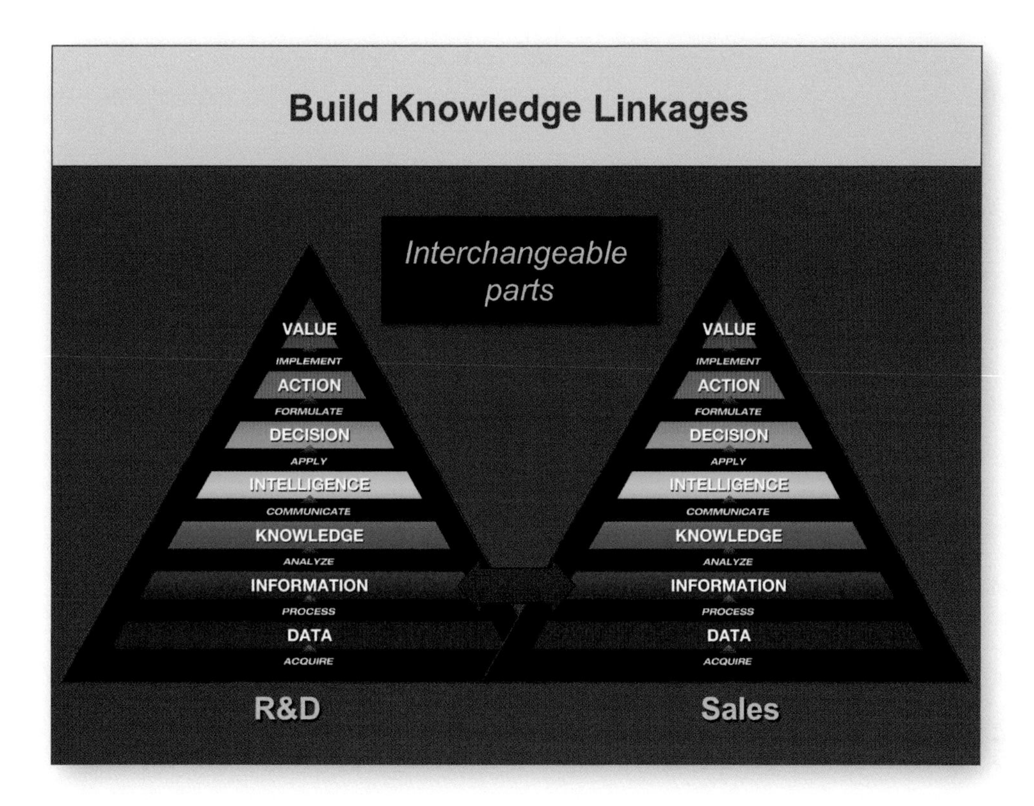

Once you build your macro view of the various KVC processes, you can begin to see where they might fit better than they do now. Again, this can be viewed as analogous to a manufacturing problem. When a large auto maker, for example, wants to cut costs, they typically go through their manufacturing process and identify where various components—a particular part, for example—can be used in another model. ***Interchangeable parts*** is a manufacturing concept that we can use to build knowledge efficiencies.

CASE EXAMPLE

In one pharmaceutical client, we discovered that R&D research data on competitive products were found to be equally useful later in the product life cycle, during the sales cycle.

We created an organizational conduit that allowed the same information to be used in both places for both purposes. In effect, an ""interchangeable intelligence part" was identified and deployed.

Intelligence "Points of Pain" 4

- **SYMPTOM:**
  "We have lots of data… but no time to sufficiently analyze it."
- **KVC LOCATION:**
  Analysis
- **TYPICAL CAUSES:**
  - Insufficient project management
  - "Firehose" data collection
  - Client impatience
- **POTENTIAL SOLUTIONS**
  - Choose your analysis wisely
    - Many techniques are situation-specific
  - Allow adequate time for processing and analysis
  - Backtime from deliverables milestones
    - Allow time for production and Quality Assurance
    - Use critical path thinking
  - Manage client expectations

Sometimes raw data are rushed into the decision process, without benefit of the processing and analysis. The unfortunate result is that decision makers end up doing their own analysis, a task for which they may have neither the time, the inclination, nor the training.

The typical cause is that relatively too much time is spent by the producer on data collection—causing him to fall behind within a fixed project deadline. So the producer rushes the analysis.

To be fair, it's often hard to predict how much data you'll find, because "research is a blind date with knowledge." If you knew up front everything you would find, it wouldn't be valuable research.

The KVC model may help sharpen the awareness—within both producer and user—that successive states are involved and that each state needs to be included. You need to budget time and other resources for processing and analysis, and to agree with your client—in advance—about these milestones. This is the best safeguard against being rushed at the end.

Project management tools (for example, software) could possibly help you here. Getting trained in some basic project management techniques may also be valuable.

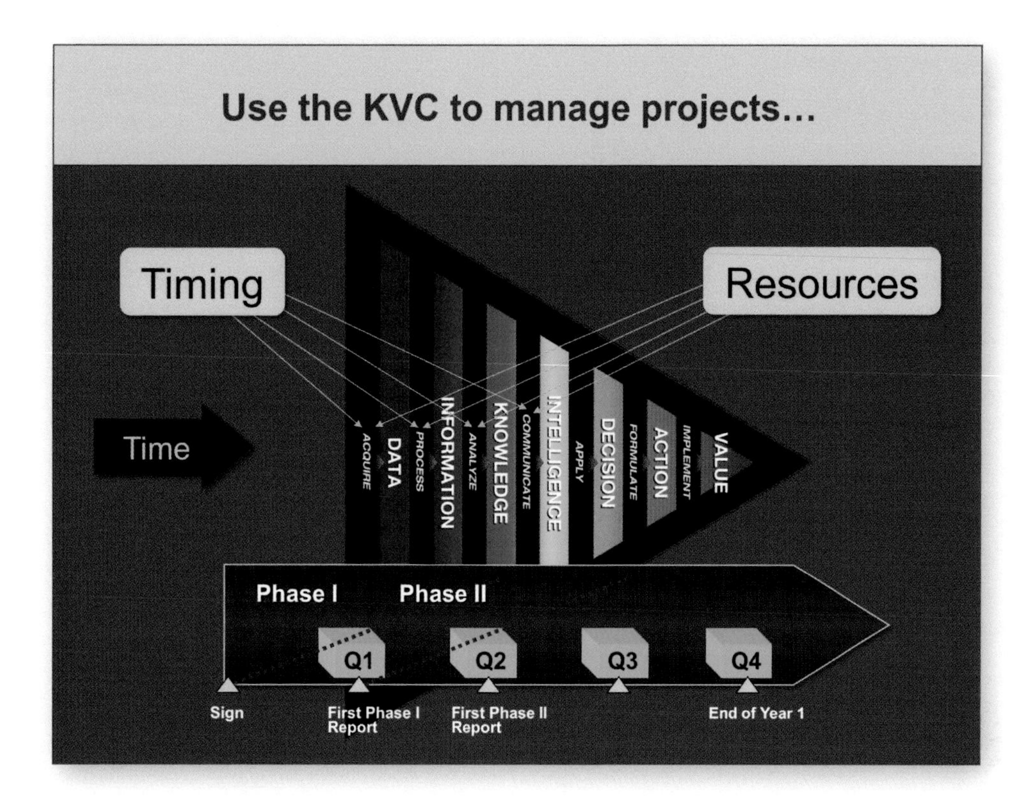

If you turn the KVC model on its side, with its pointed tip to the right, it vaguely resembles a Gantt chart, or project timeline. Each step requires calendar time to execute, and resources such as labor, time, and out-of-pocket spending to complete.

Good project management requires that each step have a budget for human and other needed resources; timed milestones and elapsed times; and responsibilities clearly assigned and communicated for both execution and management of each step.

Whether you formally use the KVC in a project management system, or informally use it to demonstrate that a defined sequence of things must happen, it can be useful in keeping projects on track and in managing client expectations.

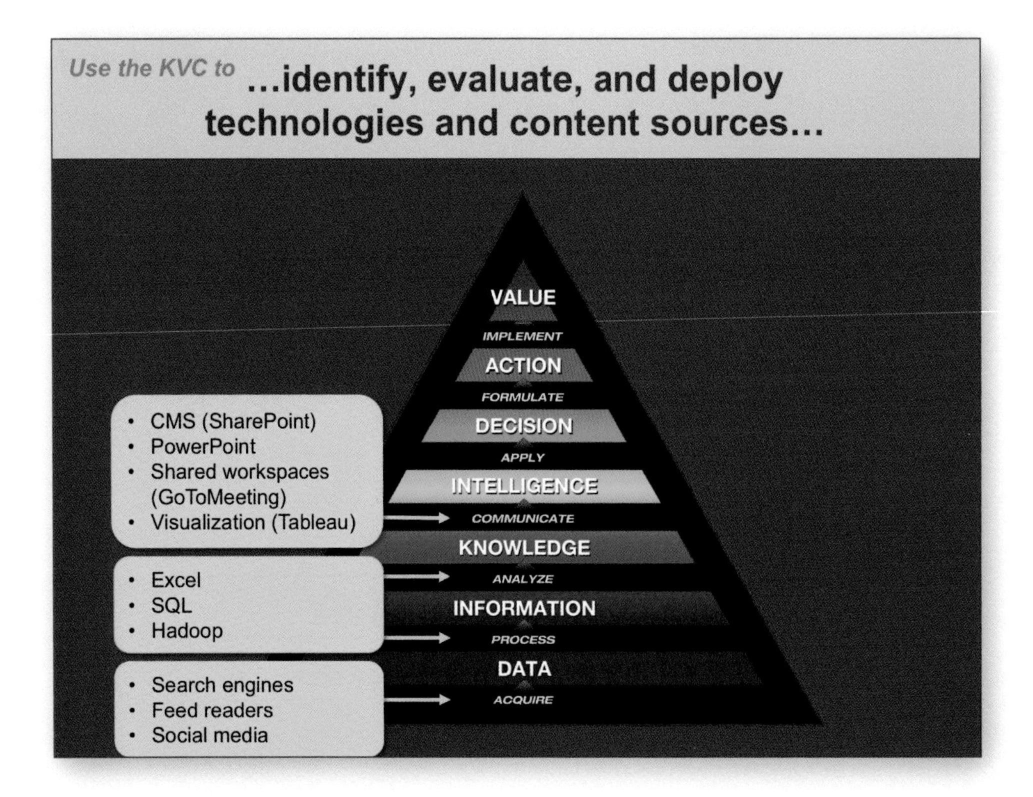

There is a range of technologies available to support various steps of the KVC. It's important to have a clear picture of where each technology you evaluate fits in the chain. Conversely, the KVC might help you see where a technology has limited application, or where another technology would serve better.

Content management systems (CMS) and SharePoint, for example, can add value at the communications step of the cycle. They can also be used also as part of the data acquisition process from internal sources (for example, sales people).

Data sources can also be evaluated in this way. RSS feeds, for example, can be useful as data acquisition tools—but then must have some value-added processing and analysis overlaid before they are truly useful in producing intelligence.

Analytic tools are in transition. Large-scale interactive databases ("Big Data") are becoming more prevalent, and the tools to analyze them constitute a highly competitive growth market. Whole new approaches like *visualization* are being developed, which help reduce massive data sets to humanly comprehensible scale.

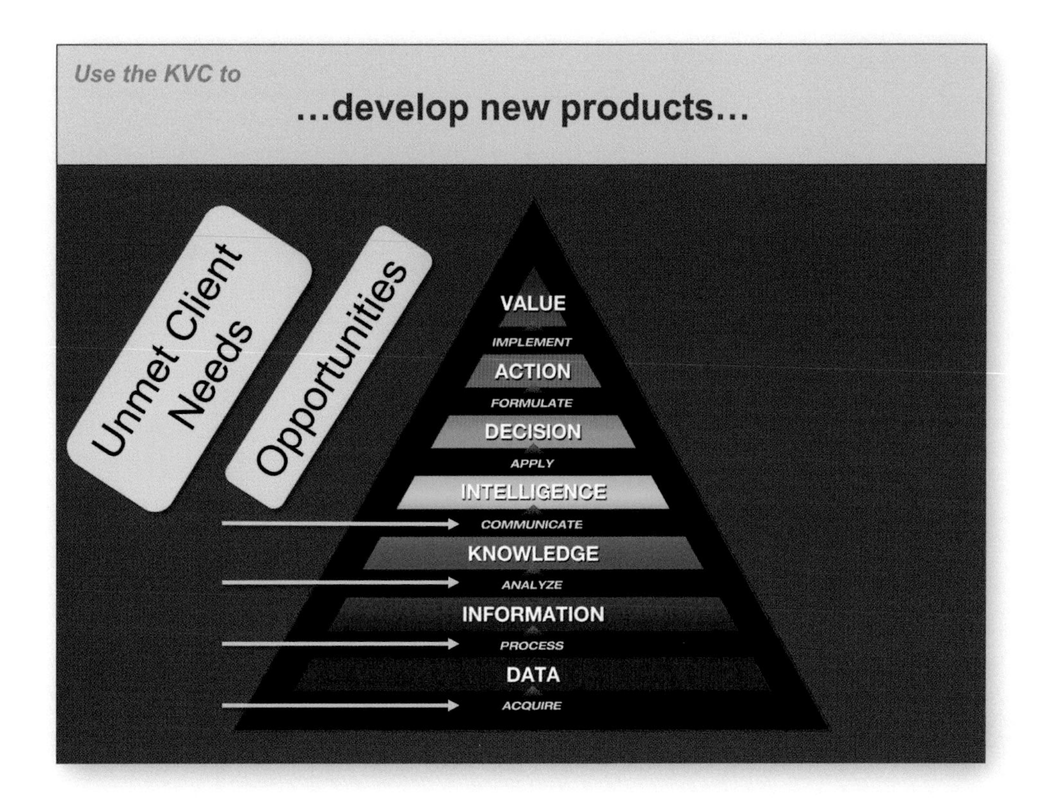

A value-adding knowledge professional is both a user/consumer of certain information products and services and a producer of others. When you wear your knowledge producer hat, the KVC can help you spot opportunities to innovate based on unmet client needs in the respective KVC segments. This can lead to acquiring an available solution, or creating a new solution.

CASE EXAMPLES

A TKA client for whom we had been an outsourced provider of intelligence for more than a decade realized that our team had more immediate access to the intelligence than their own people did. They asked us to produce an electronic repository to house our reports and other work products. It in effect it would create a seamless client workspace for our results.

We developed a proprietary content management system called SKOR™, the Strategic Knowledge Online Repository. It contained the same information we had transmitted to the client previously, but added much greater value due to its online availability and comprehensiveness.

TKA later produced a similar research repository for another large company using Microsoft's SharePoint platform.

Another client, a start-up company, used the KVC model to demonstrate to potential investors how their new information-aggregation product would add value to their customers at two specific steps of the KVC.

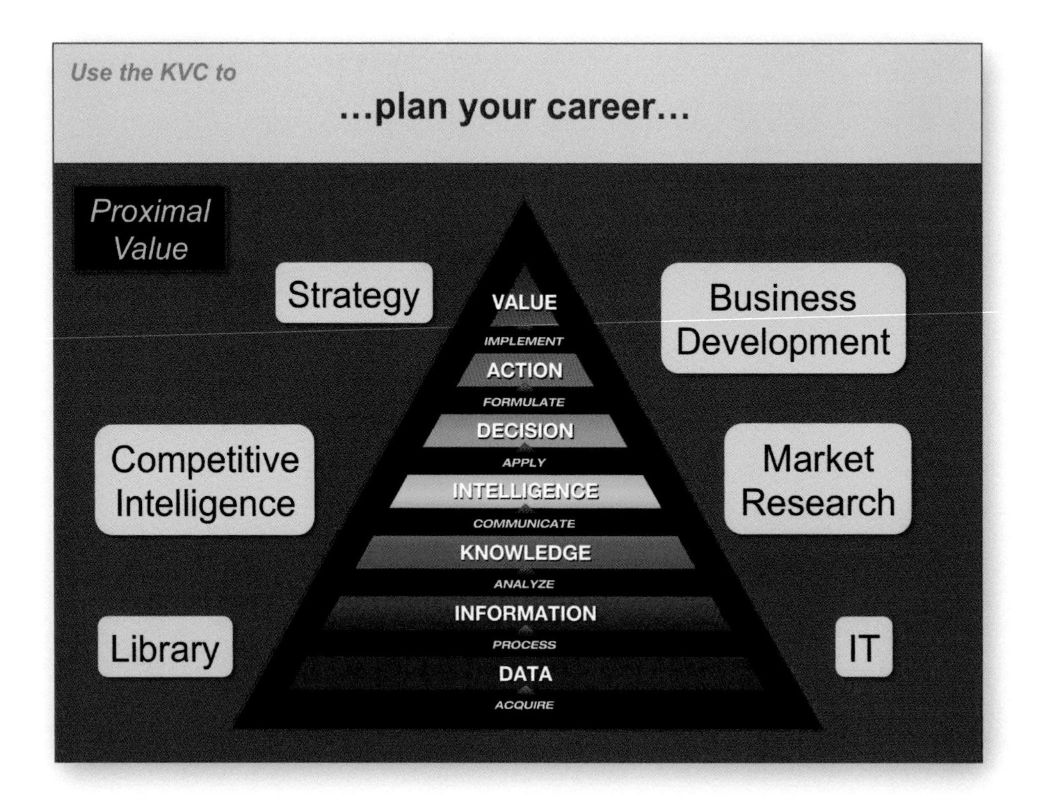

SCIP Fellow Arik Johnson proposes that each knowledge professional map his own career trajectory on the KVC continuum. Where certain disciplines (for example, IT and library science) tend to gather at the *data* end of the chain, others (for example, business development and strategy) gather at the *value* end. Corporate intelligence and market research typically fall between these extremes.

We've observed a phenomenon we call ***proximal value***. This means that the closer you are to the value production part of the chain, the more value you tend to generate professionally—at least, it is perceived that way. Greater value production tends to result in greater compensation and professional flexibility.

When library science practitioners ask me what they can do to become more valuable professionally, and I reply, "Get an MBA," I'm not kidding. If you are trained in a data discipline, the best way to advance professionally—and distinguish yourself from your peers—is to educate yourself in the value parts of the chain.

The best solution might be a hybrid academic degree that integrates elements of information science with value-production awareness. TKA's intelligence clinics attempt to do this using a concentrated approach.

Does it work the other way around? Should those value-production experts at the top also become more familiar with the knowledge parts of the value chain? Absolutely! It helps them become better managers of the intelligence process, better users/consumers of intelligence products, and gives them an edge over their own professional peers.

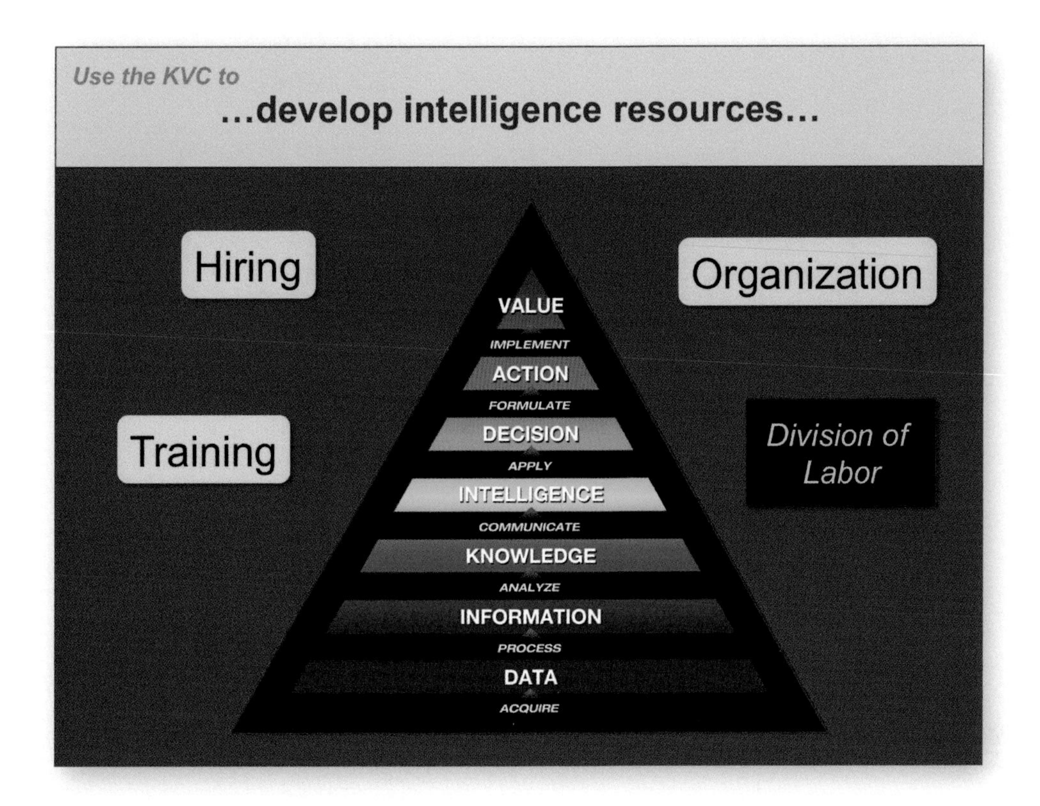

A smaller intelligence unit tends to be run like a *job shop*—where one individual or small team completes all steps in the intelligence process.

If you're managing a larger, complex intelligence operation, on the other hand, you'll be aware of the benefits of ***division of labor***. A larger intelligence group may have people who specialize in data acquisition, others in analysis and interpretation, and still others in communications. They may work more like a factory, where each assignment passes through several different groups at different stages of processing. (See the diagram on the next page.)

Where roles are separated, hiring the best people for each role becomes critical, as the skills and training needed at each step are somewhat different. Additional training and professional development can be used to fill in some of these gaps.

Project management and workflow software can help with project tracking and assuring that handoffs between groups are handled effectively.

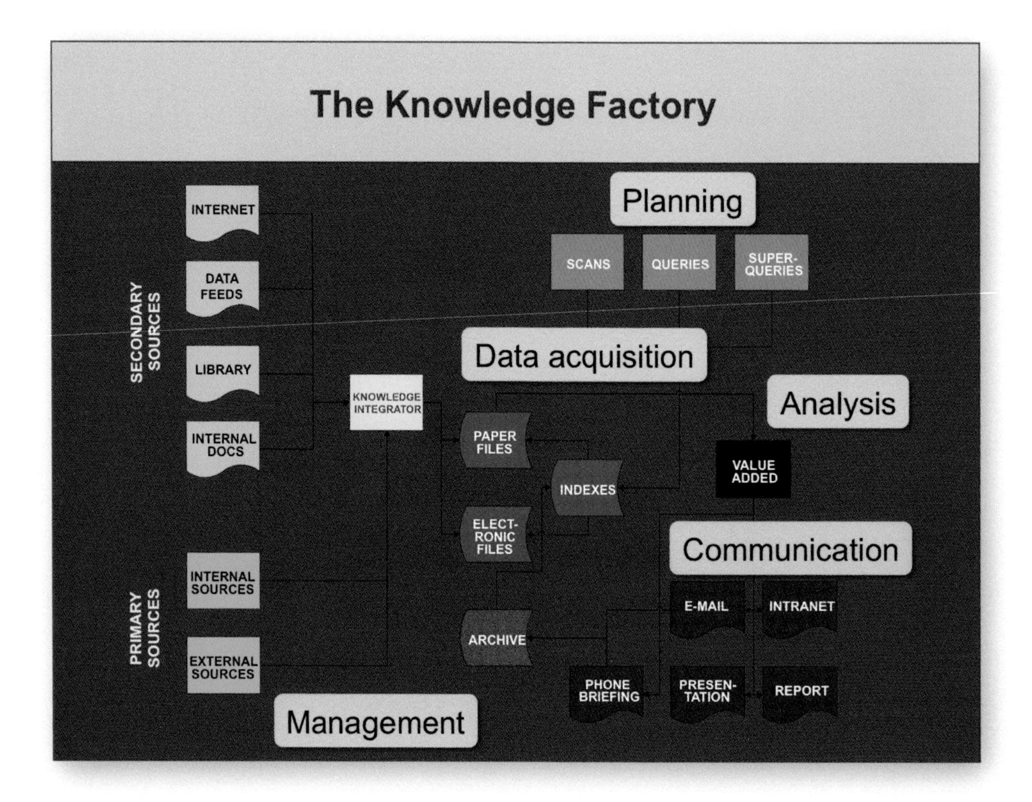

This is a high-level flow diagram of a large information center in which I once worked. We had more than 300 people on site serving more than 2,000 companies and other organizations.

The colored flow chart was produced first without use of the KVC categories (in orange), which were overlaid later. The structure of both knowledge resources and of the organization itself closely reflected the various elements of the KVC.

Much smaller intelligence operations have most of the same elements, though they may be more integrated and less staff-intensive.

Many intelligence operations, even of very large organizations, are outsourced or *co-sourced* using external suppliers to some extent. This keeps headcount low while insuring that top intelligence resources are available when needed.

When evaluating contractors, differentiation along the value chain may be evident. Certain firms may be focused on data collection, others have strengths in analysis, others are strongest when actually recommending (or even implementing) actions.

You will be able to better utilize hired resources if you:

- clearly identify your outsourcing needs along the KVC continuum;
- evaluate potential suppliers' strengths and weaknesses along that same continuum; and
- position them at the spots in your own intelligence process that best matches your needs with their capabilities.

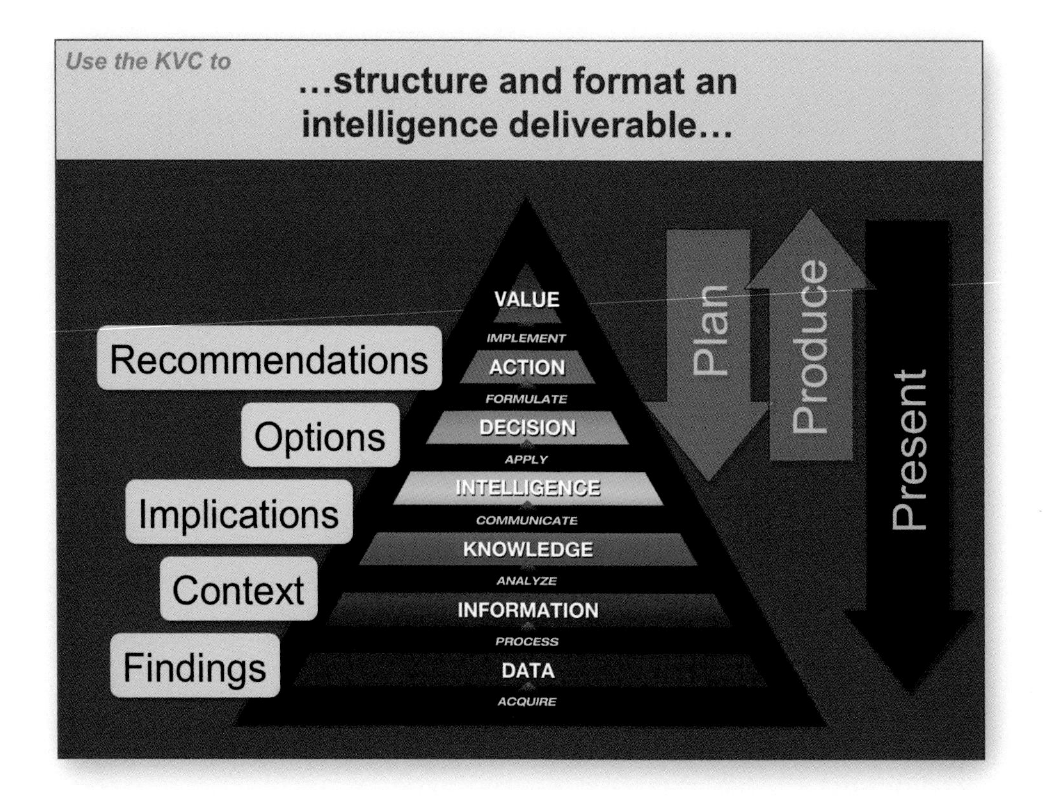

The various sections of a thorough intelligence report mimic the KVC steps. The ***Findings*** section contains the data collection approach used, the data itself, and an analysis of the data. The ***Context*** section puts gives it background and meaning in a decision-relevant framework. The ***Implications*** section communicates to the decision maker what this means "for us," and what we might do about it. Several ***Options*** might be presented—three is often a good number, reflecting best case, worst case, and most likely scenarios. Finally, a single option may be highlighted as a ***Recommendation***, based on stated decision criteria and assumptions.

The order of ***presenting*** the intelligence to the decision maker/client need not be the order in which it was ***produced***. In fact, we recommend that presentation proceed in the opposite order as production. Present your value-focused recommendation first, then the options you considered, then your analysis and how it led to that conclusion.

Hold the data and data acquisition methodology for last, even in an appendix. They should support—but not interfere with—the flow of your value-centric narrative.

This approach is consistent with most modern experts on business writing and presentation (for example Barbara Minto's *Pyramid Principle).*

The KVC is a tool for building value into knowledge processes from the data level up. But it's even more powerful when planning and evaluating intelligence and knowledge initiatives from the value level down. This approach can be used at the intelligence ***product*** level; at the ***project*** level; or even at the enterprise ***process*** level.

Each major knowledge process that an organization operates should be periodically reviewed and calibrated for its contribution to enterprise value and ROI. If, for example, a firm spends billions of dollars per year on research and development, what return on investment is harvested from new products developed and commercialized as a result?

Sometimes a whole industry operates by established metrics that are no longer optimal for its current environment. *Moneyball* is the story of how professional baseball reconsidered the standard metrics it had long used to evaluate players, found them lacking, and developed new metrics (Sabremetrics) more responsive to the changing realities of the business.

Big Data initiatives are currently at the "big promises" stage of their *hype cycle*. But tangible payouts will need to be forthcoming. One way to greatly increase the probability of this is to design such initiatives from the *value-down* perspective.

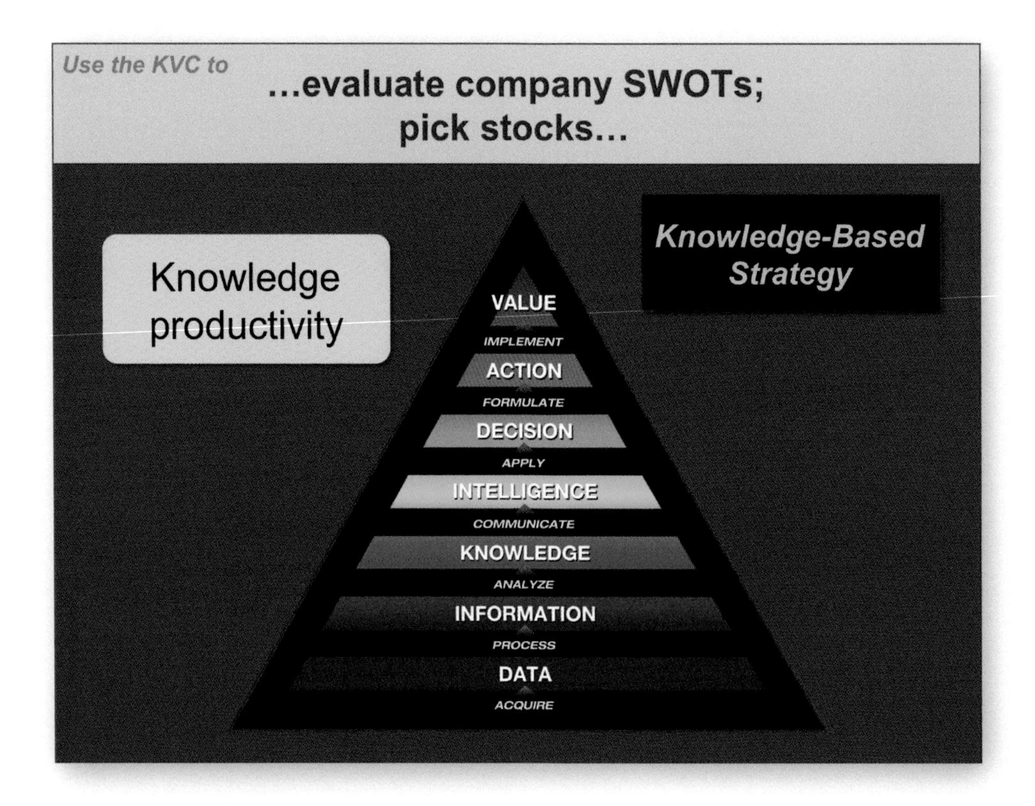

In one of his last books (*Management Challenges for the 21st Century*), Peter Drucker said that the competitiveness of business enterprises going forward would be determined by their ability to become more productive at generating and using knowledge. Ironically, however, there are few widely accepted metrics for knowledge productivity (though there are efforts underway to develop them).

Metrics aside, some fundamentally new approaches are being introduced in the ways in which companies develop enterprise knowledge. For example, in his book *Open Innovation*, Henry Chesbrough describes how leading companies like Procter & Gamble are using a networked, permeable approach to R&D innovation—rather than the "fortress" approach used by P&G and most other companies during most of the last century.

You can compare companies at a strategic level (*Strengths, Weaknesses, Opportunities, Threats*) on how well they manage knowledge-based processes. This is especially true in knowledge-intensive industries such as pharmaceuticals and consulting. We call this ***knowledge-based strategy***.

Advanced companies base their acquisition strategies partly on buying other companies with *knowledge assets* such as intellectual properties (brands, trademarks, patents, etc.) At least one mutual fund firm (Ocean Tomo) invests in companies based on their portfolios of knowledge assets.

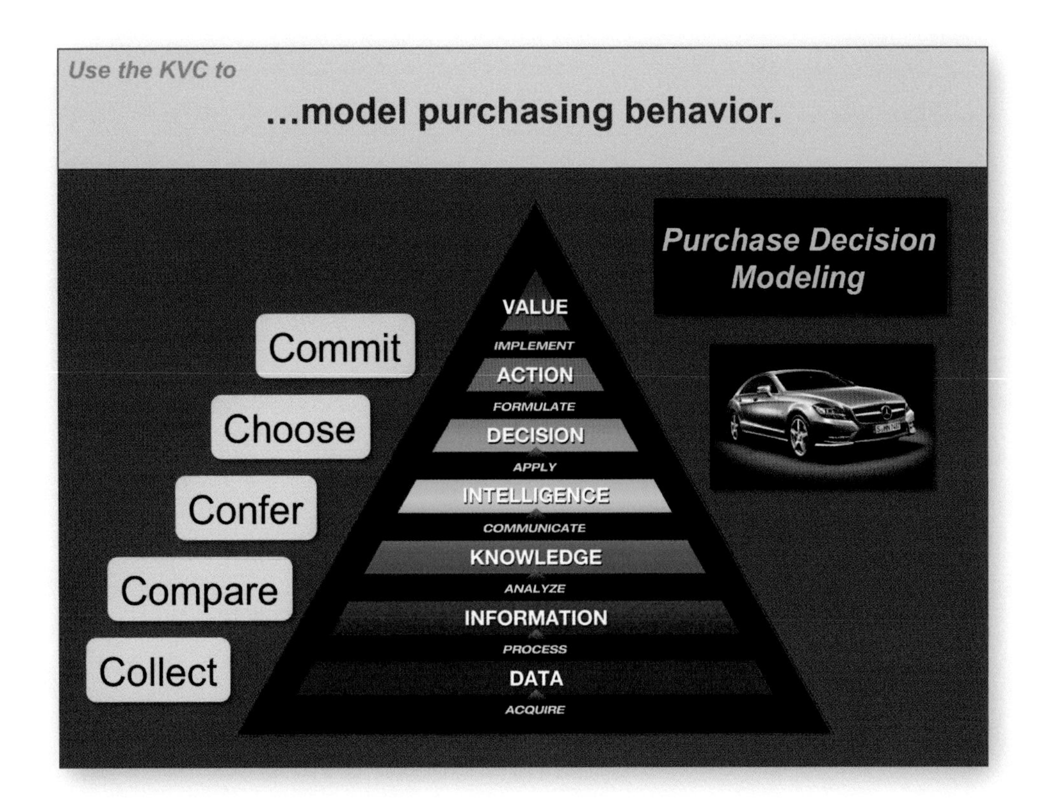

We've been discussing how large, complex organizations use information to make decisions. What about small, simple organizations, such as a family buying a new car? This is a strategic decision for many families; it requires a relatively large outlay of funds, over a relatively long time horizon.

When I recently bought a new car, I later realized I had subconsciously gone through the KVC steps. I started by collecting *data* on car models—talking to friends and neighbors; reading newspaper and magazine reviews; reading web sites and owner forums; going to car shows; and taking test drives. Then I compared various companies, models, options packages, warranties and service agreements, and even dealerships I might have wanted to purchase from. This is *analysis*.

In my family, a decision of this magnitude is a group decision, because more than one person will be using the car, and our family budget will be affected. So there was some conferring (*communication*) between my wife and me to be sure my preferences reflected her needs too.

Finally, I made a choice (*decision*) and a firm commitment (*action*) by signing a contract of sale with a dealer.

Marketers who model and understand their target buyers' purchase decision processes can discover how to use information more effectively to influence those purchases (***Purchase Decision Modeling***.)

If you are participating in a KVC Clinic, this section typically introduces Day Two of the clinic. Here we discuss how the KVC model can impact problems and challenges at the host company. We turn the KVC itself from knowledge into action plans that will result in value for your organization.

If you're only reading the book, you could stop here. But I recommend you flip through the pages and review each key lesson for:

- how it might *apply* in your organization;
- what *challenges* and problems it may surface; and
- what potential *solutions* it may suggest.

Some Lessons Learned

- Knowledge and intelligence are not the end of the chain
  - *They are "inputs" to another set of things that need to happen*
- Great intelligence does not guarantee great results
  - *There is no prize for the best information*
- A failure at any point breaks the chain, promoting failure at later stages
  - *Garbage in, garbage out*
- Focus on things that create value in ways that create value
  - *Balance process effectiveness (KVC) with strategic relevance*
- Intelligence and knowledge must contribute to the strategic goals of the organization
  - *And be measured accordingly*

Whatever your path from here, I have some take-away thoughts that I hope will stay with you.

Despite what many knowledge and intelligence producers think, knowledge and intelligence are not the end products of the chain. They're really raw materials for another part of the chain—that of the knowledge user.

Intelligence neither substitutes for nor guarantees results; that's because the intelligence can be used poorly, or not used at all.

Any link in the chain can break, leaving all subsequent steps useless or damaged.

The two fundamental paths to increasing intelligence ROI are "doing things right" (process quality, effectiveness, and efficiency) and "doing the right things" (strategic relevance).

Strategic relevance requires that the effectiveness of intelligence be measured consistently with the strategic outcomes of the organization—not by some unrelated or isolated set of metrics.

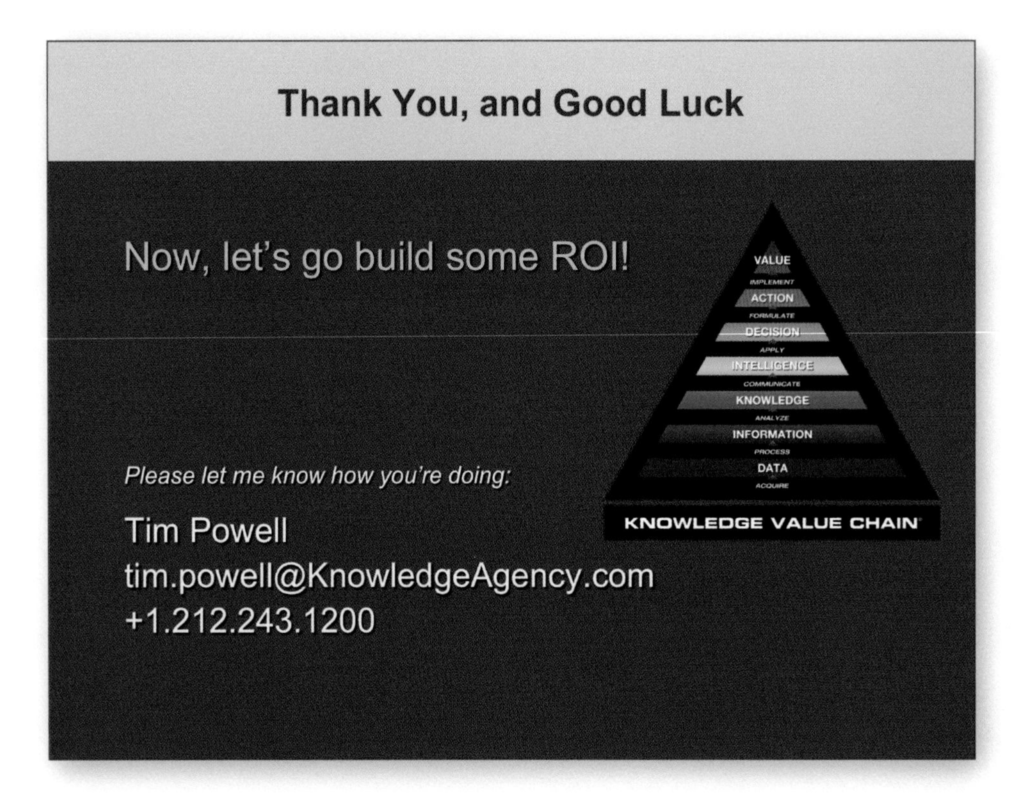

If you have questions about the KVC model or how it can be applied, feel free to contact me by email or phone.

I also collect stories of how the KVC has worked for others, and new ways it might be successfully utilized. If you have examples of where it was used and didn't work, this would also be helpful as we continue to develop and refine our approach.

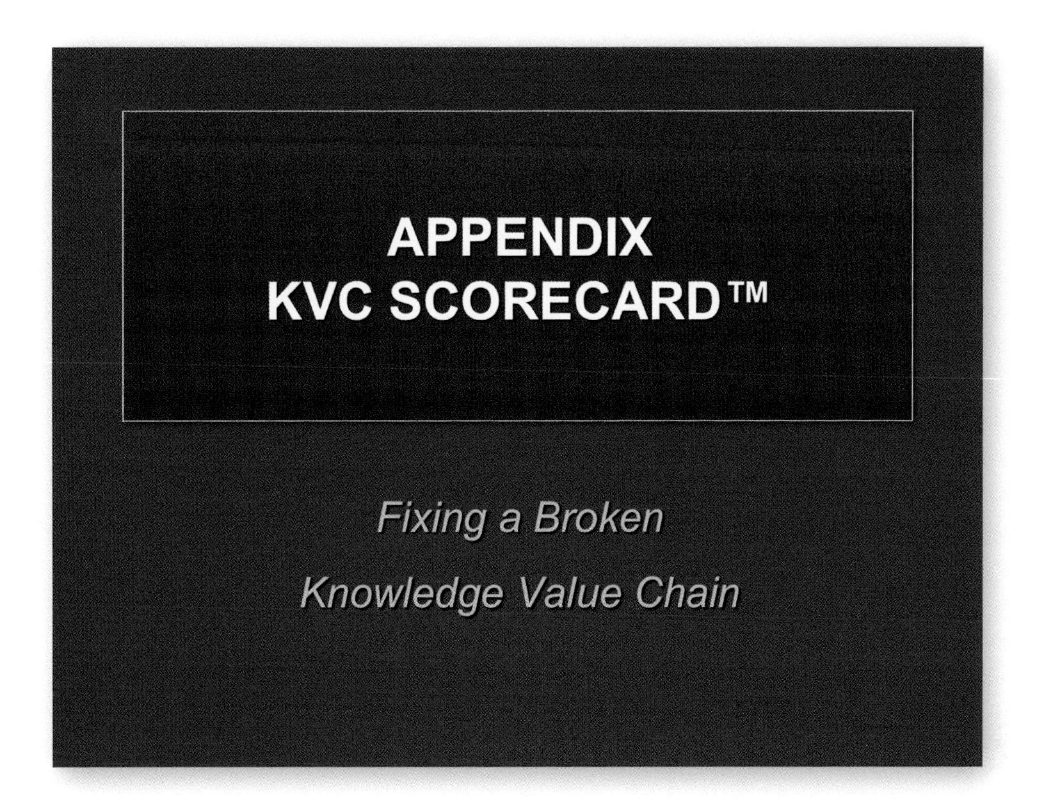

The KVC Scorecard™ gives detailed guidance about possible improvement steps at each stage of the KVC. We will explain how it works and give you sufficient guidance so that you can implement it yourself.

For each KVC Transform, there are two slides in the following section. The first contains *Value Positives*—things that if executed will increase the value of the entire process. The second contains *Value Negatives*—things that should be avoided.

The first step is to identify the intelligence problems you are having. We do this by confidentially polling and discussing with intelligence producers, managers, and users.

The next step is to identify where your intelligence problem falls on the KVC. Sometimes it's not completely clear, and it could fall into either of a couple of categories. Just do the best you can.

Once you map your problems to the KVC, you can then review the respective KVC Scorecard checklist in the following pages to identify specific potential solutions.

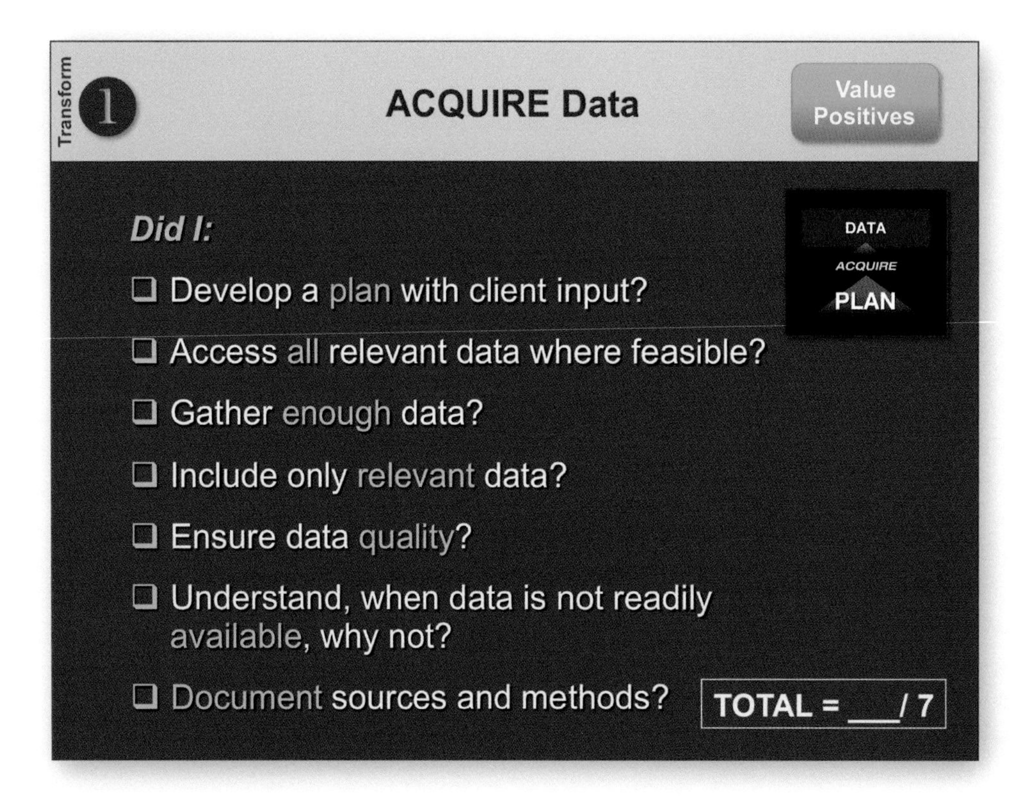

Your first value-enhancing move is for you and your client to plan what data are to be collected, what analysis will result, and how value is expected to result from the whole effort.

Be sure you access all relevant data within the scope and resources of your project. I typically start projects by identifying who already collects the data I want, and then I try to access it through that source.

How much data is enough? There are statistical tests for quantitative data, but not for qualitative data. Judgement and experience are the best guides.

Be sure you have data that is relevant to the value payout driving the effort. The Internet makes it easy to splatter your report with facts that are simultaneously true and off-point. Make sure you have a logical argument and the facts that support it—then edit the rest out.

Criteria for data quality include non-redundancy, accuracy and representativeness, relevance to the situation, timeliness, and exclusivity. To measure the value of data, these benefits are weighed against the costs in terms of cash outlays, time, and the human resources needed to manage the data.

Where data is not available, why is this—and how will I get around it?

Documenting sources and methods is key to both maintaining quality and to demonstrating quality to your client.

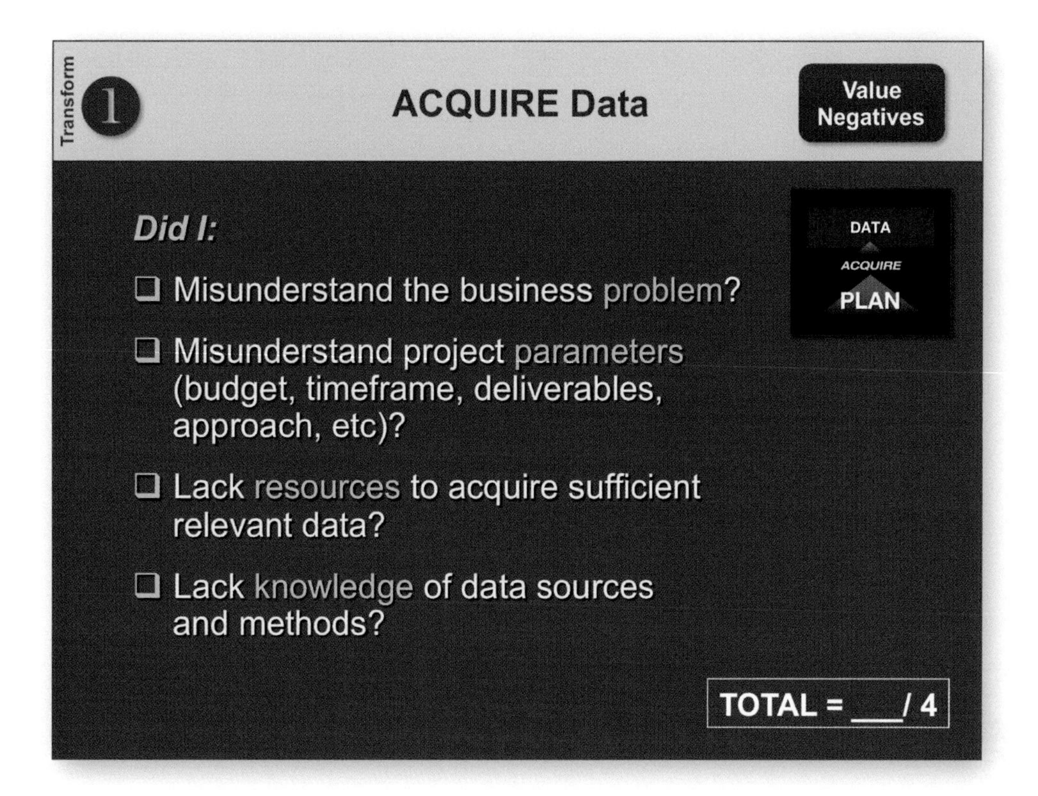

If you fail to create value at the data stage, it's often because you collected the wrong data—which, in turn, is because you misunderstood the business problem. Or you may have misunderstood the project parameters—budget, time frame, deliverables, approach, etc. In either case, a good project plan will help avoid these problems.

Resource constraints often become an issue. If you get to a point where the budget is exhausted but there are more data you think would be useful, go back to the user to see if an adjustment can be made. Be prepared to defend the value trade-off in your proposal.

It's also possible data collection was a problem because you didn't have sufficient knowledge of or training in these resources. Professional development is available for you.

CASE EXAMPLES

TKA's Points of Pain research shows that a common problem is the lack of information on private companies. You will need to talk to more people or use 'comparable' public companies as proxy data.

Another common challenge is getting information from key internal sources, such as salespeople. One approach here is to deputize them so their contacts become your contacts. This takes training and relationship building with your sales force—an investment that can pay you back many times over.

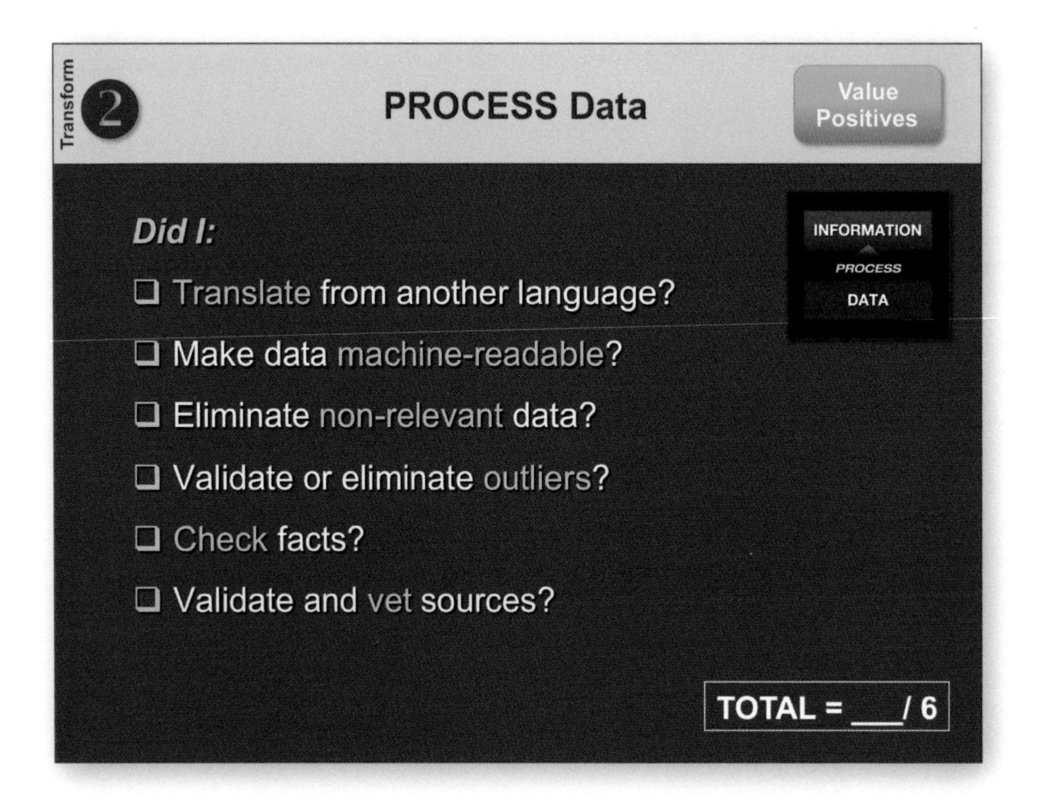

Most people want to jump directly from data collection to analysis. But that's like trying to paint a house without scraping and cleaning it first. There is preparation that must be done first. It's often dirty and not much fun, but it will jeopardize results at higher levels if you skip it.

You may need to translate data from another language. (For web sites, Google Translate can be amazingly effective.) You may need to put data into Excel or some other electronic format.

Cleaning data is a big part of processing, for example eliminating data that turns out not to be relevant, and data that seem so far out of line that they're likely in error. Errors do happen, but also you need to make sure you are not throwing away accurate data that simply varies widely from the norm.

As in journalism, fact-checking is critical in any form of organizational intelligence. The Internet has become a great collection of good information, misinformation, disinformation, unfounded rumors, myths, and outright lies. You need to be able to figure out which is which.

Discerning among sources is key here—which ones are reliable and well informed? Which ones have a hidden agenda? Which ones are simply playing back what they've heard from someone else? Vetting sources through third parties is one productive technique.

Triangulation is often useful—finding the same answer through two independent sources. But it's key that they be truly independent—otherwise you're just hearing one source with an echo.

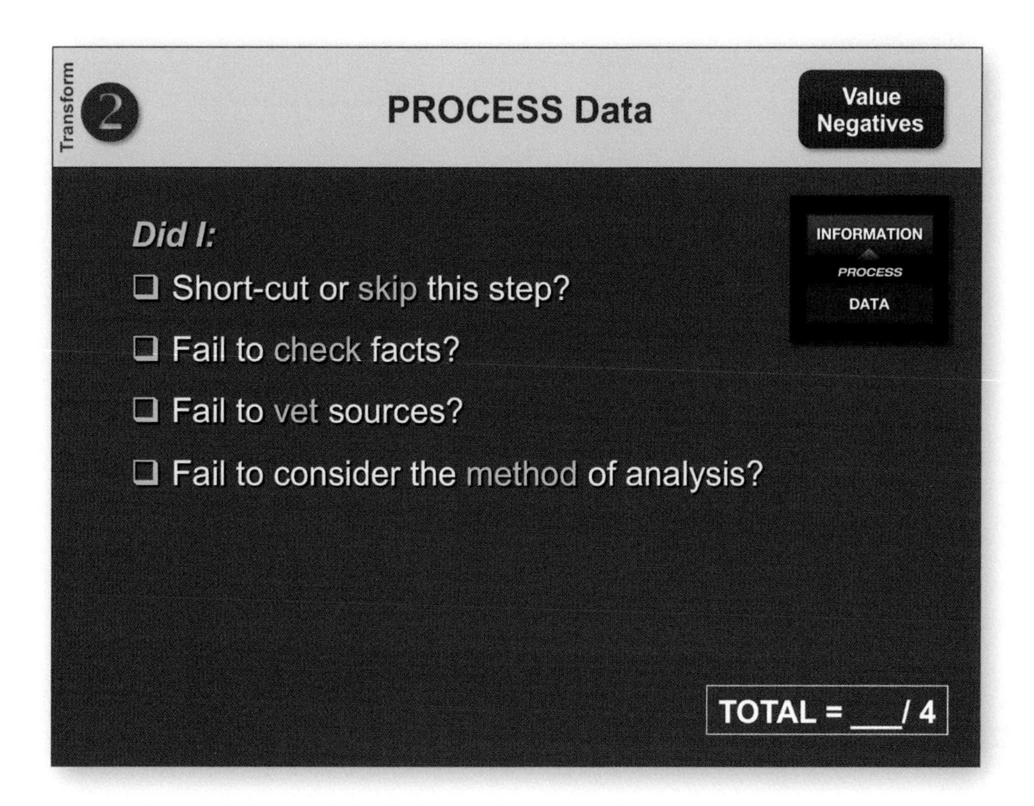

The most common value destroyer in processing is simply not doing this step at all. If you failed to complete any of the positive steps on the previous slide, you may be at risk.

You need to be sure the data is turned into a form that can be used in the analysis you want to use. Despite your best efforts at value-down planning, you may find the need to tailor the data to a form or format where it can produce the analysis you need.

CASE EXAMPLE

The most common Point of Pain complaint is the need to "weed through the morass of data to find the one or two nuggets," as one analyst put it. And with Big Data looming on the horizon, this situation could get worse before it gets better. The good news is that various new software categories are being developed to take up some of the heavy lifting.

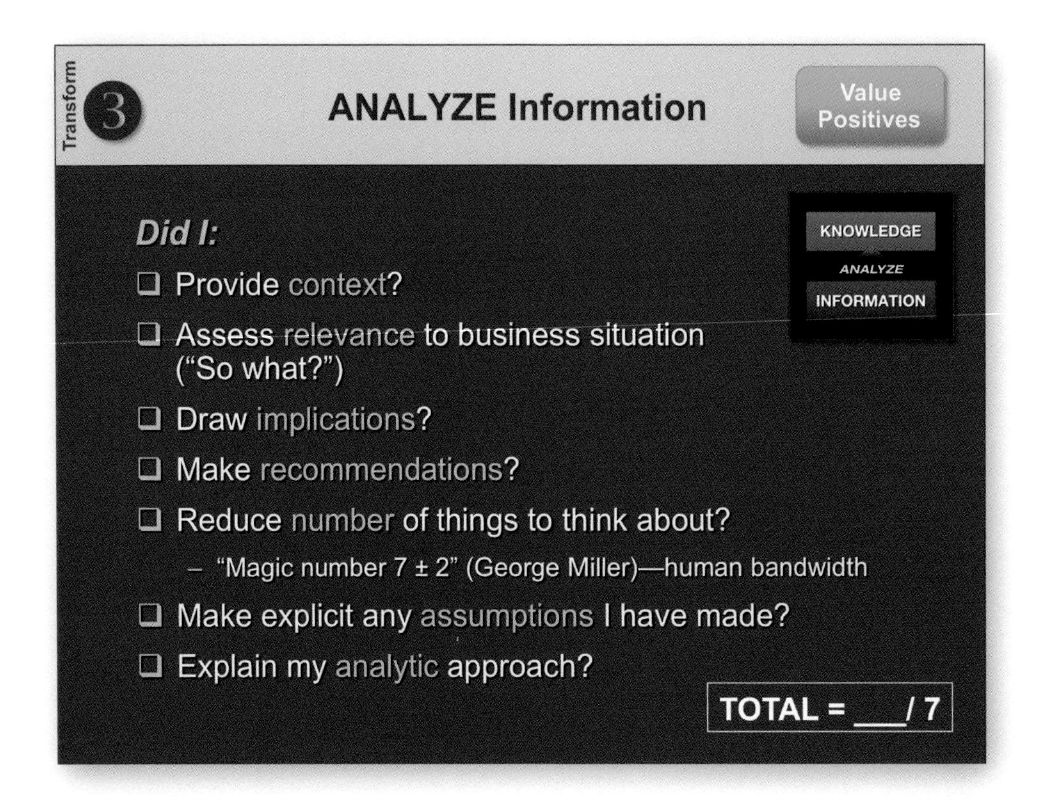

Analysis is the last stage in the production phase of the KVC—and usually the analyst's last chance to create value.

There are many types of analysis, and descriptions of them are beyond our present scope. They all require certain value enhancements to perform at their peak effectiveness.

One way to do this is to create the context and background for what is to follow. What is the "so what" relevance to the client's business situation?

What are the implications from what you found going forward? Have you made these clear?

Have you made recommendations? (Note that this is not always seen as part of the analyst's responsibilities. It's a responsibility that must be earned over time.)

Most intelligence user clients are not looking for more things to read, discuss, and think about. Many of them feel overloaded as it is. One way to help is to condense and reduce the number of things they need to worry about. But, again, this requires some sophistication on the part of the producer—and commensurate trust in him on the part of the user.

It is often necessary to make simplifying or clarifying assumptions in an analysis. These must be spelled out clearly to preserve the credibility of the entire analysis.

The analytic approach must be made clear to the client, and she must be comfortable with it.

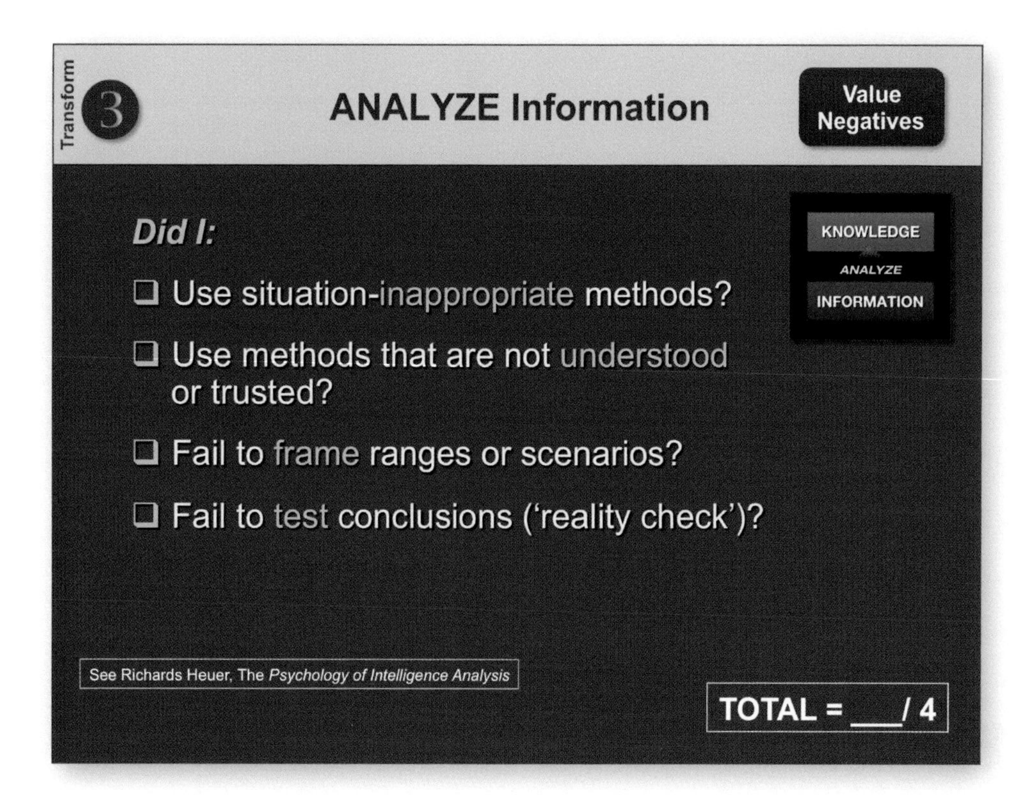

An analysis can fail because its design was inappropriate—it either did not fit the data, or it did not fit the value framework of the entire project. Or both.

The availability of analytic "cookbooks" is a mixed blessing. While they put powerful tools into a wider range of hands, sometimes these hands do not have the skills or training to effectively wield these tools.

Sometimes the tool is fine as an analytic tool, but it fails as a communication tool. Techniques, however robust, are seldom welcomed by clients if they're not part of the corporate culture.

Framing your conclusions is essential. For example, if you're presenting your results in a three-scenarios format (high, low, most likely), explain the full characteristics of each scenario.

When you reach your final conclusion, make sure it meets a "gut check" of credibility. Spiffy methods and analytic rigor notwithstanding, it has to make sense. If it doesn't, go back and find the error or assumption that threw you off.

> **CASE EXAMPLE**
>
> *I once did a sophisticated line of business analysis for a client, showing him three variables (revenues, growth, and profitability) on a two-dimensional chart. My secret, of course, was using a bubble chart.*
>
> *I was proud of my analysis—and disappointed when he explained that "We don't use bubble charts here."*

Dick Heuer's *Psychology of Intelligence Analysis* is an excellent guidebook on the pitfalls of analysis.

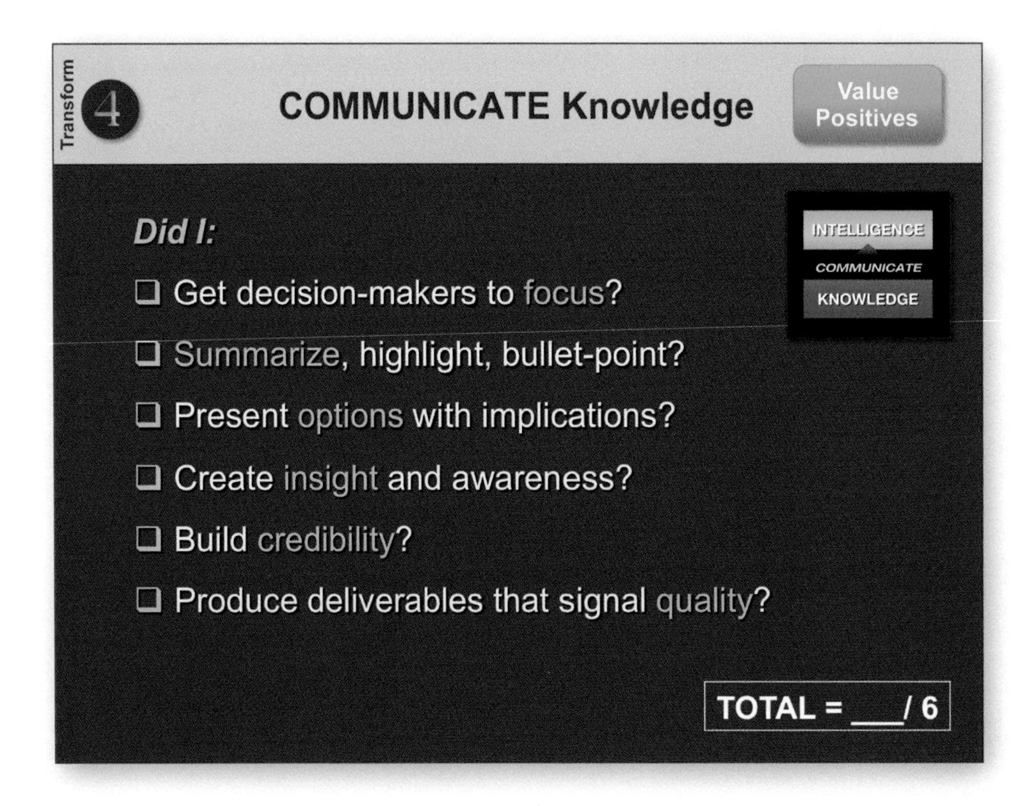

One of the biggest challenges in ***communication*** is getting the attention and focus of the decision group. Use the tips on page 82 to build a value-down deliverable that captures and holds their attention.

Build momentum throughout by using visual elements such as summaries, highlights and callouts, bullets, tables, graphs, illustrations—anything (within reason) to break the potential monotony of the report, whether it's written or oral. Use a good balance of statistics and stories to engage both the head and the heart of the listener/reader.

Always present *action-aware* intelligence. Use options to drive toward decision and action. Your job is to create insight and awareness, not just to deliver your findings.

Along the way you can build credibility for your findings by skillful use of facts and citation of sources. Don't overdo it, though—you're writing a management brief, not an academic paper.

Signals of quality are important. Be sure to have the report edited (by a second person if possible). Typos signal a sloppiness of work quality that will cause otherwise good content to be questioned.

Attractive formatting assures your audience that your product is professional. Even choice of typefaces can make a subtle difference. Don't hesitate to build in newer technologies, such as audio and video.

Communication represents the handoff of knowledge from a knowledge professional to a decision maker. There the knowledge becomes intelligence that can then be used to make decisions and take actions. Getting this step is critical to the entire KVC process, as a failure here jeopardizes the use of the intelligence product.

There are many ways this step can fail to provide the required value. One of the most common (and most natural) occurs when, in an effort to build credibility, the knowledge producer over-delivers with detail on findings and/or process. Sometimes this works. Typically, though, it signals to the user that the producer did not really understand what was important, and so he adopted a "boil the ocean" approach in the hope of finding something relevant.

This is a question of setting the *gate value* properly, so that mainly signal is communicated with little noise. This is especially difficult because different users may set different gate values. One may want to be notified the current *status* of a situation each day; another may just want to be notified when there is a *change* in the situation.

CASE EXAMPLES

Common Points of Pain challenges include building credibility among users; getting management to act on findings; being seen as more than a library or repository; having work claimed by others higher in the hierarchy; understanding user challenges and needs; and building buy-in when findings run counter to conventional management thinking.

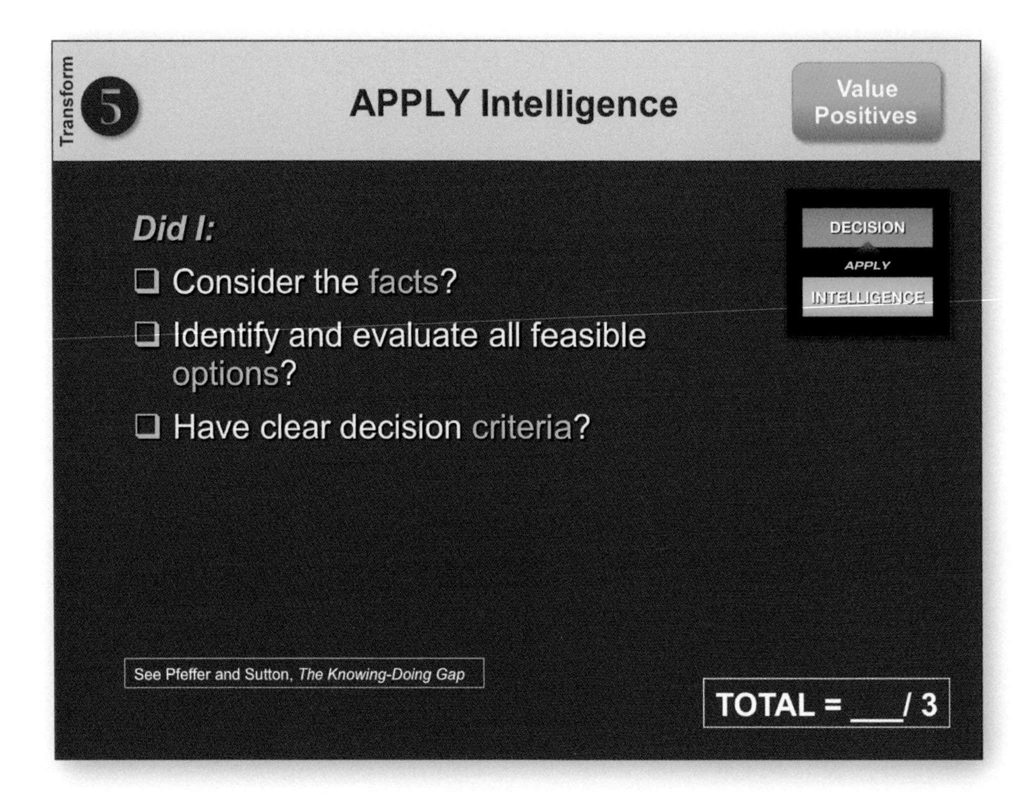

A competent job by the intelligence producer will make the intelligence user's task much easier. Making decisions based on good intelligence is what many decision makers were trained to do, especially if they had formal training using the case method.

Decision making is as much art as science, especially when a group of people is involved. As shown on page 61, in addition to formal intelligence, there are informal sources of intelligence, and even non-related *externalities* that can interfere.

A common problem is that a sufficient range of options has not yet been explored. Generating options may or may not be part of the intelligence team's formal tasks. Even when it is not, the user team should verify that all feasible options are being considered.

A common fail point here is that *decision criteria* have not been identified or agreed upon in advance of applying the intelligence. Where this happens, intelligence may be used to back-fill criteria at the same time that a decision is being made—not an ideal situation.

Pfeffer and Sutton's *The Knowing-Doing Gap* is an excellent practical guidebook for turning knowledge into action in a complex organization.

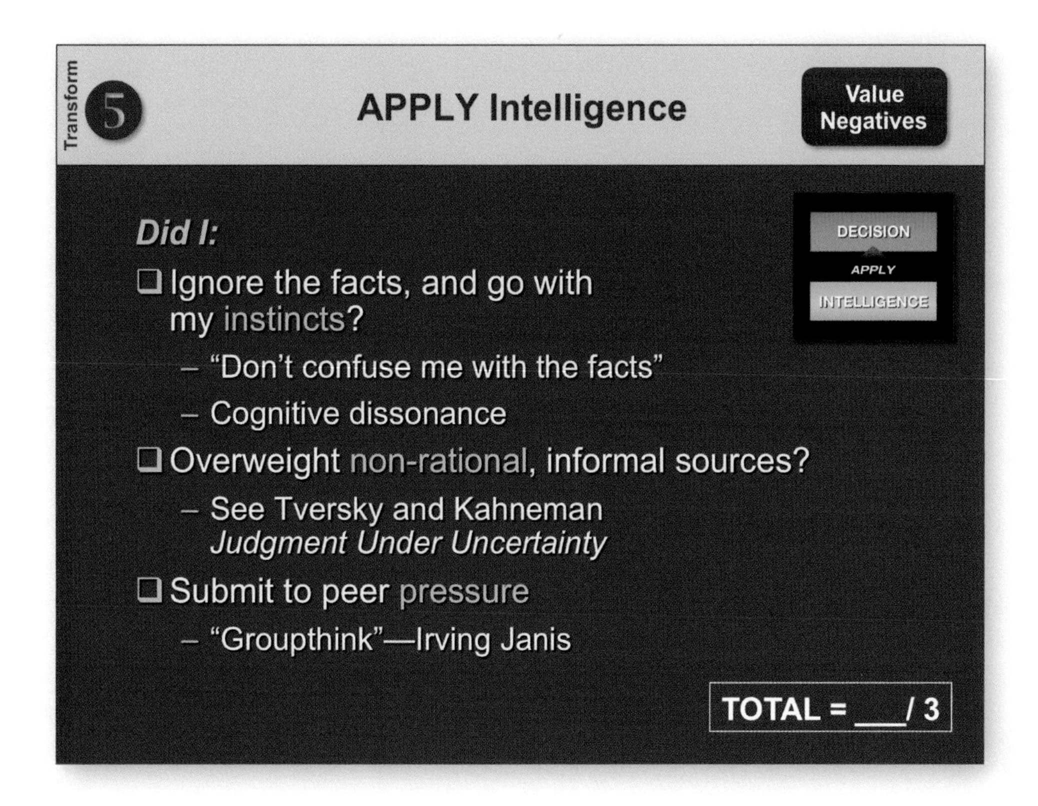

Decisions made counter to intelligence recommendations happen all the time. Why?

Confirmation bias is the tendency for information seekers to put more credibility on information that confirms what they knew already, rather than seeking information that calls their beliefs into question (which creates *cognitive dissonance*).

There is a large and growing body of evidence that supports the claim that "rational man" has hundreds of ingenious ways to make decisions irrationally. This goes back to a paper published in the 1970s by Tversky and Kahneman that describes the *heuristics and biases* that affect most decisions. This insight has become the cornerstone of the field of behavioral economics.

Group dynamics can either improve decision making or make it worse as *groupthink* takes over, and individuals become reluctant to break ranks and express their own opinions. *Consensus* is a powerful political and social tool—but there is a downside if people fall into unquestioning acceptance of the group will.

As General George S. Patton said of his command leaders, "If everyone is thinking alike, then somebody isn't thinking."

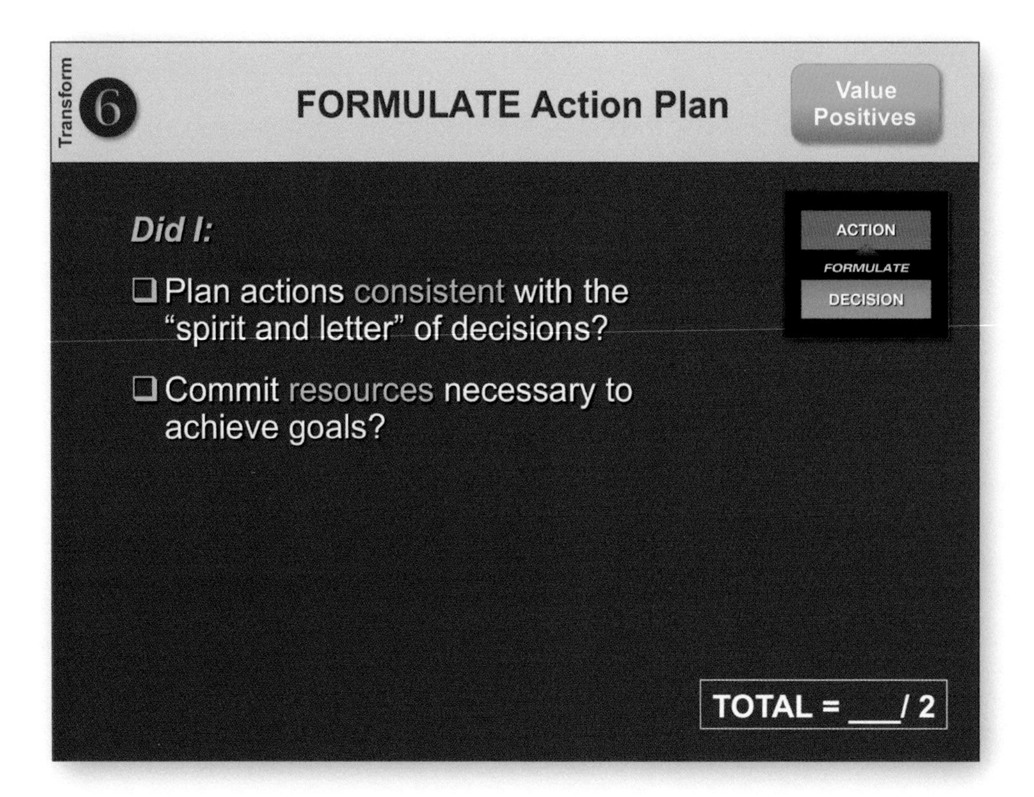

The implementation team often has to do a great deal of interpretation of the decision to make it work.

A key potential fail point during implementation planning is the resource budget. Budgets may be provided along with the action plan, or they may require a separate appropriation of funds. In either case, lack of resources is the surest way to cripple or kill any implementation effort.

Making decisions is a lot more interesting and fun than making them *work*. There is a tendency, once a major decision is made, for management to lose interest as they move on to the next thing.

The project must be handed off to an execution team. If the project is not delegated adequately, with clear accountability and milestones, things can then go into a sort of *implementation purgatory*, where they get stuck—sometimes permanently.

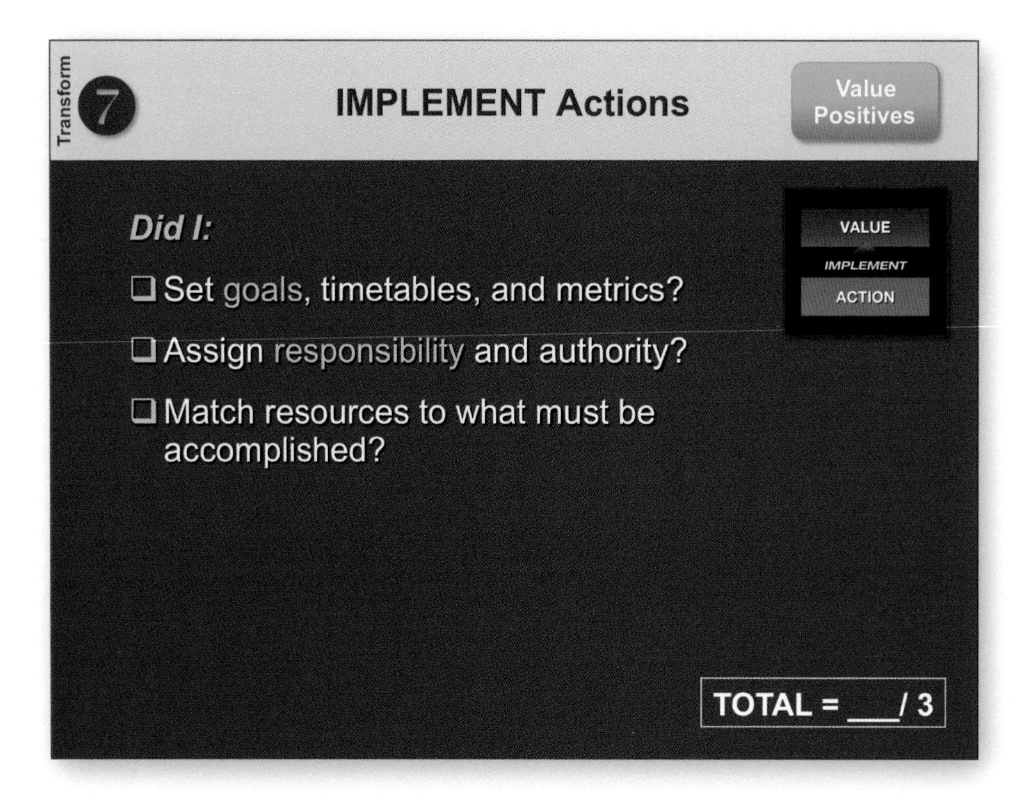

Implementation of a decision is largely a matter of project management. In many cases the management team will delegate the decision to a task force team for implementation.

Resources (budgets and people) must be brought online at the right times to get the desired result. Timetables and milestones must be planned and executed. Responsibilities and reporting relationships must be established and maintained.

Before one of his fights, prizefighter Mike Tyson was asked to comment on his opponent's reported plan to outmaneuver him. Tyson's reply was, "Everybody has a plan until they get hit. Then, like a rat, they stop in fear and freeze."

The same is true of organizations. Adverse events encountered early in the implementation phase can cause momentum to be lost. It's management's job to determine whether the unexpected adversity is due to poor planning, or to new events that it was impossible to foresee. In either case, it may be necessary for the implementation to be modified before further execution is considered.

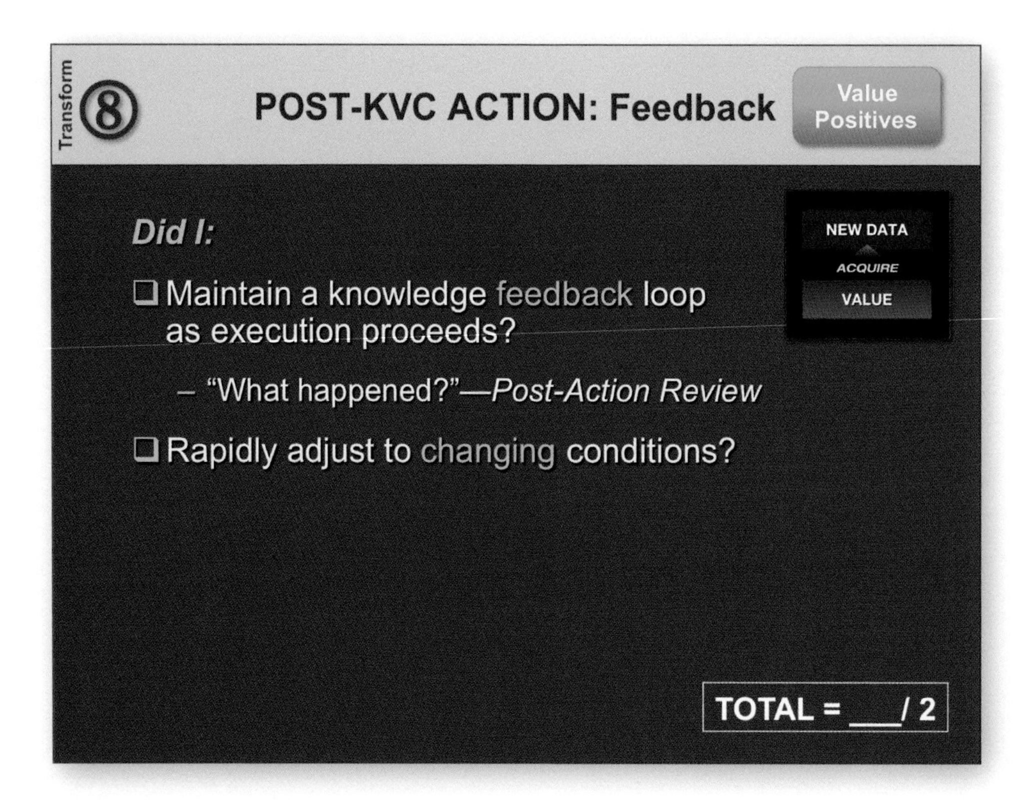

Nineteenth century military strategist Helmuth von Moltke said, "No plan survives contact with the enemy." He described strategy as "a system of expedients."

It's much the same in business. We should *not* expect our plans to survive the first contact with the real world; on the contrary, we should *count on* their not surviving intact.

One key to a successful strategy is revising your original plans quickly as you develop new information generated by engaging with the real world. The world changes quickly, and adaptive flexibility and resilience may be equally powerful as foresight and planning.

Do this review of *what happened* consistently and objectively, rather than on an ad hoc basis. Post-action reviews and post mortems are ways to achieve this.

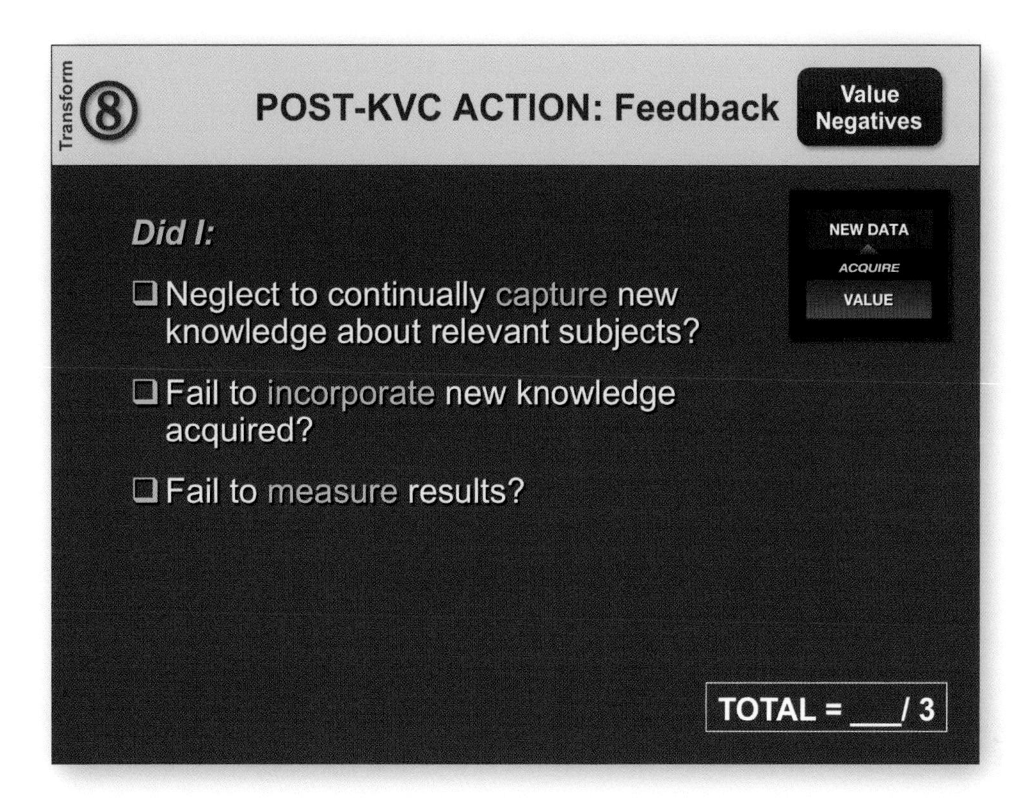

Sometimes this feedback effort gets lost in the shuffle because it's no longer strictly either research or implementation. When it's no one's job in the organization, it may easily fall between the cracks. As a result, you can fail to capture this new information, which is typically even more valuable than that captured before implementation.

Your organization's sales force is an especially good source of information about your products and strategic initiatives once they are launched in the marketplace. Building internal intelligence networks with top salespeople is a key value-adding activity that can provide great rewards.

KVC Scorecard

KVC STATE	Value Positives	Value Negatives	Perfect KVC Score	Our KVC Score
DATA	__/ 7	__/ 4	19.6	
INFORMATION	__/ 6	__/ 4	16.8	
KNOWLEDGE	__/ 7	__/ 4	19.6	
INTELLIGENCE	__/ 6	__/ 10	16.8	
DECISION	__/ 3	__/ 3	8.4	
ACTION	__/ 2	__/ 1	5.6	
VALUE	__/ 3	__/ 2	8.4	
FEEDBACK	__/ 2	__/ 3	5.6	
TOTAL	__/ 36	__/ 31	100.8	

You can use the ***KVC Scorecard*** to rate an intelligence report, an intelligence process, or even a whole intelligence function. Take the number of checks you received under *value positives,* then net out the number of *value negatives.* A perfect total score would be 36. If you prefer this *normalized* to a 100-point scale, multiply your result by 2.8, as we've done in the table above.

The formula for this is:

KVC SCORE = (Vp - Vn) * 2.8

where Vp = the number of value positives

and Vn = the number of value negatives

You can see exactly where you fell short by comparing your net KVC score to the total possible KVC score for each section. Then you can look back at the slides for each section to suggest actions to correct the problems you've identified.

The Knowledge Value Chain®: How to Fix It When It Breaks

Revised version of a paper originally presented at KnowledgeNets 2001, New York City, May 2001, and published in M.E. Williams (ed.), Proceedings of the 22nd National Online Meeting. Medford, NJ: Information Today, Inc.

Abstract

This paper applies the "value chain" model developed by Harvard Professor Michael Porter and others to knowledge-based processes. Parallels are drawn between knowledge development/application and other value-added processes such as manufacturing. As in manufacturing, the Knowledge Value Chain is described as a series of *States* (stages of processing), with a series of *Transforms* required to move from each stage of processing to the next. An example involving the highest levels of strategy in a major US firm is described. Various implications of the model are drawn, including those that use the model to diagnose common problems in the development and application of knowledge.

Background

I had recently joined the Board of the Society of Competitive Intelligence Professionals (SCIP) when I was approached by a new member, who was also new to the field of competitive intelligence (CI). She asked me, "What do CI people actually do?" I began explaining to her the value-adding transformation of data to information to knowledge, and finally the communication to someone with the authority and power to do something about it (a "decision maker"). I advised her that thinking of it like any other manufacturing process would help demystify the process, and give her a grounding in the "real world." Then I began to diagram, on the back of an envelope, the beginnings of what later became the Knowledge Value Chain.

An early version of the KVC was published as the "Business Intelligence Value Chain" in my chapter "Analysis in Business Planning and Strategy Formulation" in Gilad and Herring's compendium *The Art and Science of Business Intelligence Analysis* (JAI Press, 1996). The first time I used the term "Knowledge Value Chain" to refer to this model was in a workshop I presented in 1998.[1]

Introduction

Virtually all of us reading these words are "knowledge workers"—in doing our jobs, we read articles and journals, search databases, talk to people, think about and summarize what we've found, and communicate our findings to decision makers. But the *process* by which this occurs is not well-defined or understood, either by cognitive scientists or by business process experts. Yet the knowledge-creating process stands at the heart of modern organizational competitiveness.

We must understand the knowledge process before we can attempt to improve on it. We must peer into the "black box" of knowledge work and attempt to see what is inside, and how it works. Why? Simply put, the productivity of the knowledge worker is seen by experts as the single most important factor in the competitiveness of the modern organization.[2] And productivity is best enhanced when work processes are broken into their basic elements.[3]

We must find some way to turn *information* into *business value*. Stated that way, this transformation sounds magical, like the transformation of lead into gold that the medieval alchemists struggled to achieve. Their quest, though ultimately futile, was not entirely in vain; as a by-product it seeded the body of knowledge that eventually became modern chemistry. That's because the alchemists developed a systematic process to document their tests and findings, and to catalog and share these findings.

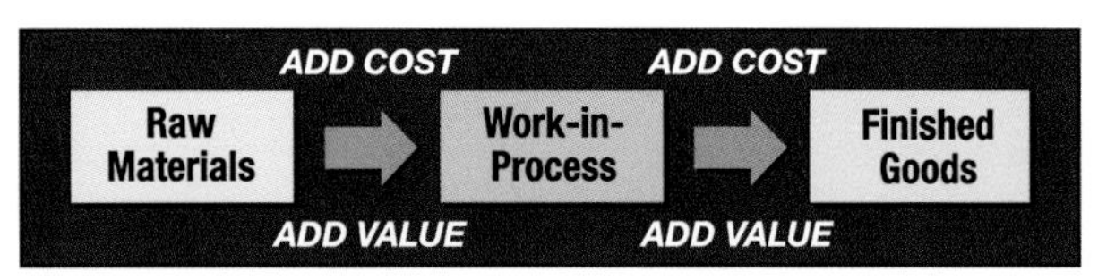

Figure 1: A simple manufacturing value chain

Definitions

In defining the Knowledge Value Chain, we need to define each term that goes into it. Let's start in the middle, and work our way out.

Creating value is ultimately what organizations are all about. In business, we measure value by a number of metrics. These include:

- financial measures (for example, revenues and profits;stock price (also referred to as "shareholder value");
- innovation (for example the number of new patents granted);
- other more complex and sophisticated measures such as the *Balanced Scorecard* developed by Kaplan and Norton, and *Economic Value Added* (EVA) developed by Stern and Stewart. These include a mix of measures such as customer satisfaction and production quality.

Non-business organizations have similar measures of effectiveness and efficiency.

The *value chain* model was popularized by Michael Porter in his 1985 book *Competitive Advantage*.[4] We'll define it here as *a series of related activities that together produce end-user benefits*.[5] A simple example of a value chain is manufacturing. Here a defined series of steps transforms raw materials into work-in-process at various stages of completion and finally into finished goods ready to be packaged and shipped.

Each stage of processing adds both costs and value (defined here as the purchase price paid by the end user). Each step should add more value than cost—and if not, that step needs to be re-engineered in some way.

A car manufacturer, for example, buys a lot of raw materials—sheet steel, various plastics, glass, rubber—and component parts like headlights, microchips, and so on (Figure 1). The total cost of these parts, plus the labor to put them all together, plus the ownership and maintenance of the factory and machines, plus the costs of the dealer network, plus all the advertising and promotions, and so on—has to be less than the selling price of the finished car. If total costs exceed the selling price, we have to re-engineer these parts or steps to cut the costs— and/or raise the price of the car. If neither of these is feasible, the car model is phased out, and ideally replaced with one that is more profitable.

The ***knowledge value chain*** is simply the application of the value chain model to knowledge development and usage. In short, it is a process model of how data becomes intelligence, and eventually becomes part of a business result or benefit. The balance of this paper will describe this KVC process.

The Knowledge Value Chain

The knowledge value chain (KVC) comprises two major sets of activities, ***knowledge production*** and ***knowledge use***. This reflects the division of labor in knowledge work that has evolved in large, complex organizations. Here, ***knowledge professionals*** are primarily tasked with knowledge acquisition and development, and ***decision makers*** apply the resulting knowledge to make better business decisions, plan and execute actions, and thereby achieve business results.

The KVC model contains an alternating series of "states" and "transforms." Each state is a *stage of processing*, a work-in-process (like a partially built car would be in an auto factory). Each transform contains actions that effect the *transformation* needed to move to the next stage of processing.

There are a total of seven process states and seven transforms. Each transform has as its "input" the state preceding it, and as its "output" the state following it. Each of the seven transforms presents opportunities to add value—or to fail to do so, or to even destroy value, if the transform is omitted or executed poorly. Each step is thus a potential ***fail point***, at which we need to determine whether we are sufficiently controlling quality.

Figure 2: The Knowledge Value Chain

Transform 0.
Plan

The KVC model (Figure 2) starts with a planning process that begins at the top of the KVC—*How will value be created?*—and goes "in reverse" down through the steps. This results in a shared understanding between the knowledge professional and decision maker as to how the effort will proceed. The quality of this step is essential to the whole rest of the process. If this part is flawed (rushed, for example—or skipped entirely), the remainder of the process cannot achieve the level of value enhancement possible.

To use our car manufacturing analogy, in some cases great expense and time are spent designing and manufacturing cars that ultimately fail in the marketplace because the "decision maker"—in this case, the consumer—does not want them. By contrast, the Honda Accord is legendary in automobile history for two reasons: (1) it was one of the best-selling models year after year, and (2) massive amounts of consumer research went into defining the car's features before it was even designed. There is a direct correlation between these two.

Likewise, a failure of intelligence planning can result in a mismatch between the intelligence process and the business goals it serves. For example, you might spend a lot of time and/or resources researching a problem that turns out not to warrant the urgency you gave it. On the other hand, something of great importance to the business could be overlooked, if that importance is not clearly communicated.

Both examples derive from a failure to achieve shared understanding at the outset. The project planning phase should produce "shared understanding" on these basic project parameters:

- the time frame;
- the budget (if any);
- the use that is to be made of the information; and
- any sensitivities that may exist around the project.

Transform 1.
Acquire Data

Then, and only then, can the knowledge worker go off and begin to *acquire* data. Data are the equivalent of "facts and figures," the points around which we will eventually build our analysis. (When we say "acquire," we are speaking of any method of obtaining data, including—but not limited to—its purchase for a fee.) This can involve speaking to people on the phone, going online, looking at printed sources, and so on. (Exactly where and how to acquire data is a long discussion beyond the scope of this paper. This is the subject of another of my books, *Analyzing Your Competition.*)

Given the proliferation of data that exists, often this step involves *selecting* and *filtering* a bounded set of data from a much larger data universe. Capturing data from Google searches into an Excel spreadsheet is an example.

Having acquired the data, the analysis can begin—almost.

Transform 2.
Process Data

Before analyzing the data, there is almost always an interim step that involves *processing*—cleaning, organizing, and otherwise preparing the data so that it can be analyzed properly. This step may involve, for example, entering data into a computer. For another example, a digitally recorded phone conversation might need to be run through voice-recognition software and entered into a word processor before it can be analyzed.

Numeric data points can be entered into a spreadsheet, and trends lines and charts drawn. Publications in a foreign language must be translated into the analyst's native tongue. Facts need to be checked and validated. Sources need to be vetted. "Outliers"—data points that lie far outside the general trend of the data—need to be examined, and decisions made as to whether they are valid and should be included, or whether they are spurious and should be dropped from the data set.

Transform 3.
Analyze Information

The processed data is called *information*, and only now is it ready to be analyzed. During the *analysis* phase, we transform information into *knowledge* in the following ways:

- by giving it *context*—what are the circumstances surrounding it?
- by assessing its *relevance* to our organization—what does it mean *for us*?
- by drawing *implications* for action—what do we recommend be done about it?
- by outlining *options* and alternatives, and
- by *reducing* the amount of information to an amount able to be understood and acted on by the decision maker.

In this fast-paced and information-cluttered world, attention and focus are two very precious commodities for even the "highest-bandwidth" decision maker. It is the analyst's job to produce both ***attention*** and ***focus***.

Transform 4.
Communicate Knowledge

In this most crucial step, knowledge that heretofore has been in the mind of the knowledge professional is transmitted to a decision maker (or, more typically, a decision-making team). This typically happens by a combination of means including emails, formal written reports, slide presentations, and personal briefings. In effect, this step reproduces (in a compressed form) the knowledge-building process in the decision makers who are at the same time grappling with some business problem. Here, though, the process must be accelerated and concentrated—and that, too, is part of the knowledge professional's role.

A successful communication gives the right amount of material, summarized and well-organized, complete with analysis, conclusions, recommendations, data sources, and any qualifications needed on the quality of the data or likelihood of outcomes predicted ("If present trends continue...", "Experts predict that...", etc.) A successful communication produces *insight* in the decision makers, and *credibility* for the knowledge professional.

This transferred knowledge is now intelligence, defined as *knowledge in the hands of someone with the capability of acting on it.* Once this handoff to a decision maker is made, too often a knowledge worker will consider the job done—and, in an active sense, this is true. But in the sense of value-production, the process to this point has not yet produced business value, since nothing has yet been achieved with the information.

Knowledge professionals who seek to improve their effectiveness benefit greatly from knowing what happens after this knowledge transfer. Only by knowing what is done with the knowledge that we give to decision makers will we be able to improve our work product and processes. Just as market researchers need to find out what happens to products once they go into general market release, the knowledge professional needs to understand the balance of the process, after he/she ceases to be directly involved.

Transform 5. *Apply Intelligence*

Decision makers do just that—often working as a team, they take intelligence, and use it to make decisions for the organization. These decisions typically involve resource allocations—where to invest, where to pull back, etc.

A key factor in any decision is when to make it. Some decisions are *time-driven*; for example, budget decisions. Others are event-driven; for example, what to do when a key executive resigns. Other decisions are neither time- nor event-driven, but are driven by change in some variable; for example a drop in sales. Lacking a pre-defined threshold condition (for example, review sales strategies if sales fall by 5% or more), these latter decisions are problematic precisely because it is not clear when they need to be made.

The process we have described so far is a formal decision-making process. Studies have shown that, while such formal processes are often involved in any major decision, there are also typically informal inputs. These can include the decision maker's former experiences, informal sources such as a spouse or neighbor, intuition, and a whole host of "externalities" such as political factors.

Significant barriers can come between the presentation of good intelligence and its application. Failures to apply intelligence can include ego ("Not invented here"), group pressure ("They all think it's the way to go, maybe they're right"), and what psychologists call *cognitive dissonance* ("Don't confuse me with the facts").

Transform 6. *Formulate Action*

We are getting closer to the end results, but we are not there yet. We need to plan and execute some actions that embody the decision. This step is a major source of "disconnects" in the KVC. For example, in the US, our lawmakers and the courts stop at decision making, and leave it to an array of federal, state, and local agencies to try to implement their decisions. Even when a good decision is made, it can be rendered ineffective by the lack of well-executed actions to implement it.

Transform 7.
Implement Actions

Now the actual implementation of the decision and resulting action plan begins. Resources must be committed, goals and timetables must be set, and some way of monitoring the results must be devised. Now, and only now, are we in a position to gain business results from our original knowledge work.

Transform 8.
Feedback

Implementation is also a key chance to gain some new data. As implementation goes forth, there is an opportunity to gather data of a typically higher quality than in preceding stages. This feedback needs to be put into the cycle at the top, and analyzed quickly in order to provide a "course correction" to the whole process.

For example, in rolling out a new consumer product, test markets are typically conducted. These are "live" product rollouts, but on a scale limited to two or three cities. The costs of product distribution and promotion are much lower than for a full-scale rollout; therefore the risks are much lower. Key things can be learned that can be "fed back" into the actual rollout—including whether that larger rollout should even take place. These include the reactions of customers to using the product and of retailers to selling the product.

Management

Though not strictly a transform, management is the glue that binds the whole process together. Management issues are addressed here as they relate to each transformational step.

A KVC Illustration

We can use the mnemonic "DIKI-DAV" to guide us through the KVC process. As an illustration, let's apply the KVC model to a company's decision to acquire another company. ***Project planning*** could include a basic definition of the characteristics of a target company of interest: industry, revenues, profitability, market share, distribution, etc. ***Data*** might include the stock price and trading volume of a potential target. ***Information*** (processed data) would include trends lines, arrays, and graphs built out of this data. ***Knowledge*** could include, correlations between the stock price and volume trends with news about the company, and with conditions in the market in general.

Intelligence would result from the analyst's bringing all of this data to the attention of a decision maker. A ***decision*** to make an offer to acquire the target company could result. An ***action*** plan would be formulated to define the terms, process, and support players for the acquisition. The ultimate ***value*** results from the impact of the acquisition on the acquirer's earnings, stock price, and market share.

Typical Disorders of the KVC

As mentioned earlier, the point of understanding the KVC process in detail is to be able to fine-tune it, and to fix it when broken. I'm fortunate to have had the opportunity to study competitive knowledge development first-hand in a range of organizations and industries. In doing so, I've been struck by the fact that knowledge workers across industries and geographies have an amazingly similar set of challenges and problems. I believe that many of these can be readily understood and corrected by using KVC analysis. Several examples follow.

PROBLEM: "We don't know what management wants." This is a common complaint of knowledge workers. This is typically a planning stage (Transform 0) problem, because there has been an inadequate dialogue between knowledge professional and decision maker. As a result, the data to be acquired can't be defined properly, and the whole chain spins off its sprockets. The reader may feel that even the word "dialogue" glorifies what is too often an eleventh-hour frantic plea for help.

POSSIBLE SOLUTION: Make sure a true planning exchange happens before data collection starts. Define the project parameters listed previously. Use a checklist so you don't forget something. As a rule, project misunderstandings are best identified up front, so they can be corrected early in the process.

PROBLEM: "We have piles of data—but never enough time to analyze it." This is an analysis (Transform 3) problem, and commonly results from the rush to complete projects. If you fail to process and/or analyze data, you will be tempted to provide unprocessed, unanalyzed data or information to a decision maker. This reduces the value of the communication, and, if done repeatedly, calls your credibility as a knowledge professional into question. You must add value though analysis—though it is always good to separately identify "the facts" from your analysis of them.

POSSIBLE SOLUTION: In planning the project, be sure to allow adequate time for processing and analysis. Back-time from the "deliverable" deadline, including the final production, and the analysis to get to the results. Always allow some "slip time," as Murphy's Law is alive and well. ("If something can go wrong, it will. If something cannot *possibly* go wrong, it will anyway.")

PROBLEM: "We do great analysis—but management doesn't use it." This communication (Transform 4) problem results when credibility has not yet been established, or the relationship with the decision maker has been damaged in some way. Creating a positive relationship and ongoing dialogue with decision makers is one of the most difficult and important challenges in any knowledge-based process. Knowledge workers and decision makers coexist across a "culture gap" that often impedes their communications. Almost everything about them is different. They typically are trained differently, paid differently, dress differently, live and work in different communities, and so on. The need for, and difficulty of, bridging that culture gap—thereby gaining trust and credibility—is often underestimated.

POSSIBLE SOLUTION: Do some "market research" with your decision maker clients. Determine what they find most effective in terms of content, format, and medium of communication. Follow up on projects—what was most useful, what was least useful, what needs to be improved.

PROBLEM: "We do great analysis—but management keeps asking for more." This is an Transform 5 problem (decision), in that decision makers may feel that they need a greater level of certainty before making a decision. As a rule, the greater the level of resources to be allocated based on the decision, the greater the level of certainty that decision makers will seek. Higher stakes require greater assurance. But, paradoxically, a good data collection and analysis effort often raises as many questions as it answers. This leads to the apparent need for more information. Typically, though, the costs and time to produce new analysis (and especially new data) are underestimated, and can impede the smooth flow of decision making. This can lead to the situation commonly known as "paralysis by analysis."

POSSIBLE SOLUTION: Raise the sensitivity to the trade-offs between greater certainty on the one hand, and greater time, effort, and budget expended on the other. Keep the flow of events moving toward decision making.

PROBLEM: "Once we go into implementation mode, we stop collecting data." The feedback loop (post-KVC) is often ignored, thereby cutting off a source of real-world validation and course-correction for the original decision. The problem may be an organizational one—the issue is handed off from a development team to an implementation team. The latter is less familiar with data collection, may not have the resources for it, and generally does not have the cultural bias toward information gathering that the research people do.

POSSIBLE SOLUTION: Create an ongoing, active communications linkage between the research and implementation teams. Encourage the feeding back of new data into the KVC.

PROBLEM: "We have many KVCs—but they don't link with each other." One key difference between the KVC process and a physical manufacturing process stems from the intangible nature of the KVC "products." In an auto factory, once a bolt has been used in one car, it obviously can't be used in other. But data and information are "non-wasting" assets—they don't get "used up" when used. As such they are infinitely reusable. Data used in one KVC can be used in another somewhere down the road—and often should be. Too often this doesn't happen due to the boundaries of time and/or organizational structure.

POSSIBLE SOLUTION: Create a macro view of the various knowledge chains in your organization. Look for opportunities to redeploy information in ways that enhance value.

Here's an example of how such "knowledge redeployment" can work. I once conducted a knowledge development workshop with a major pharmaceutical company. In one of the group exercises, we determined that the competitive product information gathered by scientists at the beginning of the drug development process stayed in the R&D unit. We discovered that many months later, when the drug had completed development, testing, and approval, the same data could be useful to the sales force tasked with moving the product into doctors' offices.

We built a mechanism to systematically transfer the same data (comparative drug effectiveness) from the R&D teams to the sales teams. Building this simple linkage saved the re-creation of the information at a later time and in a different context.

A Tragic Example

Over time, the misuse of knowledge can erode the fundamental value created by a business. A recent example, tragic in its proportions, comes from the Xerox Corporation.

Once upon a time, Xerox was considered a paragon of corporate life in many respects. They had great products, and single-handedly created the market for corporate copiers. They were also leaders in business practice. For example, they pioneered some innovative applications of information—the modern practice of product benchmarking was perfected there.

But it didn't last—it almost never does. First, the copier market was invaded by high-quality, lower-cost models from Canon and other (mostly Japanese) manufacturers. Xerox tried to reposition itself as an information technology company—right before the technology crash of 2000. After peaking at $63 in 1998, Xerox stock crashed with the dot-coms in 2000, when it traded below $4. At that time, Xerox developed serious credit problems, and was rumored to be going bankrupt.

By most accounts, Xerox's organizational misuse of knowledge is at least one key factor in their fall from grace. During the 1970s, scientists at their Palo Alto Research Center (PARC) were responsible for a stunning series of key inventions of the digital age: the laser printer (1971); Ethernet (1973); the graphic user interface, or GUI (1975); the personal computer (1977); and the portable computer (1978).[6] Yet in each case, Xerox was ultimately unable to use these inventions to create a dominant position for itself in the commercial marketplace. Its knowledge, in short, was not translated into value.

What's worse, in each case another company *was* able to do so. For example, Steve Jobs was able to emulate the Xerox Star computer GUI technology to create the subsequent breakout success of the Apple Macintosh. IBM (now Lexmark) and Hewlett-Packard took most of the share of the laser printer market. Ethernet was commercialized by Intel, Digital Equipment, and 3Com.

The core problem Xerox had was a variation on the knowledge professional–decision maker culture gap described earlier. The scientists at PARC were removed from the company's primary decision makers, both physically and culturally. The PARC scientists had a shirt-sleeve Silicon Valley culture long before it was fashionable in the East, and were driven by creativity—and even fun. The Connecticut-based decision makers worked in a button-down, bottom-line environment heavily pressured by Wall Street earnings expectations. They were skeptical of the new ideas from the Wild Westerners, and refused to adequately fund the commercial development of these key technologies. This created the opportunity gaps that other companies were able to successfully exploit.

This series of decisions not to enter new markets, overlaid with drastically changing conditions in Xerox's core copier market, created long-term strategic problems from which the company still has not recovered.

It may never fully recover.

Key Implications

Now that we understand the KVC process in principle, how can we apply it to solve problems? What lessons and implications can we draw? Some of these are as follows:

Knowledge is a linear process. In contrast to some "cyclical" models of knowledge development, KVC is a linear model. Like manufacturing, it uses a series of steps to define a final product. The key lesson here is that *you must understand the destination before you start the journey*. And that destination is not simply the approval of your decision maker client (though that may be a good real-world proxy for the true payout.) The true payout is the final business outcome that will result from the whole process.

Knowledge is a serial process. The states and transforms are "wired in series." *When one link in the value chain is broken, by definition the chain itself is broken.* A failure at any step is replicated in all later steps. For example, a great analysis of faulty data will produce a misguided conclusion. The old adage "garbage in, garbage out" makes this point memorably.

Each step in the KVC is integral and essential. If you short-circuit the process (which you might be tempted to do to save time or other resources), you will fail to create value—or possibly even destroy value. The classic example is when a decision is made without sufficient information to support it. The result is more a matter of luck than of strategic management. While it is possible to succeed in the short term under these conditions, over the long haul the odds are stacked heavily against doing it repeatedly.

Knowledge value chains interact. In the pharmaceutical case mentioned above, a single data set was employed in two otherwise separate KVCs. You need to map out these various KVC processes, formally if possible, in order to identify and improve these interactions. As an example, when you finish a project for a decision maker, it is helpful to find out who else could use the information (with, of course, your client's consent).

Knowledge creation is like manufacturing. I state this here as a conclusion, though admittedly it was more accurately a hypothesis going into this series of propositions. However, to the extent that it is true, we can then use the many insights into manufacturing that have been gathered by students of that discipline.

Manufacturing concepts that we can borrow in the study of knowledge-based processes include:

Incremental value added. Each of the seven transformational steps can be examined separately, and some assessment made of its incremental cost and value-added. Though it may not be possible to do this on a strictly quantitative basis, at least at first, the exercise will still yield important insights.

Productivity. The productivity of knowledge-based processes is a primary aspect of competitive differentiation. In manufacturing, productivity is defined as the ratio of output to input (for example, person-hours to produce one automobile), each of which can be measured relatively accurately. While the metrics for knowledge-based process productivity may be considerably more "fuzzy" at present than they are for manufacturing, the concept itself may ultimately prove just as valuable.

Quality assurance. Just as in manufacturing, quality can be built into the knowledge process. The alternative can be to find out when a complete study has been done, and resources expended, that they are the right answers—*to the wrong questions*. One form of quality assurance, for example, consists of establishing frequent touch-points with the decision maker on the project status (from both sides). This will avoid any "process surprises."

Load balancing. Too often a knowledge process is off-balance in terms of resource assignments. A common example is that too much time is devoted to data collection, and too little to analysis and communications. Load balancing enables you to identify and clear the bottlenecks that may be dragging down the whole process, and to reallocate resources in order to clear those bottlenecks.

Just-in-time (JIT). JIT manufacturing came into practice because there is a cost of inventory associated with each raw material and purchased component. This cost is, typically, the financing cost of purchasing the item, plus the cost of the physical warehouse space in which it is kept. For information, the inventory cost is typically not the "warehousing" cost—that's almost negligible, outside of the costs associated with hard drives and other media.

The main cost element associated with information is its *obsolescence cost*—its inexorable tendency to become continually less representative of the "real world"—hence less valuable—over time. The world changes constantly, while information often does not. Any piece of produced information begins to "decay" as soon as it is produced. Some information decays rapidly—"Who wants yesterday's paper?", as the song goes—some less rapidly.

As a result, it is useful to consider "just-in-time" knowledge—the production of knowledge at the last possible moment—to minimize the risk of obsolescence. (Maybe all those last-minute information requests serve some economic purpose, after all!)

Inventory. The view of information as a highly perishable asset raises other considerations. These issues include which information we should keep "in inventory"; which we should produce on demand; what is the current value of the information we have in inventory; etc. The nature of the inventory can vary; for example, a current list of sources may prove nearly as valuable as having the sources themselves—assuming those sources are readily retrievable when needed.

Auditing. Physical inventories of raw materials, work-in-process, and finished goods are periodically subjected to structured verification processes called *audits*. Your knowledge inventory should be, too. In this way you can determine what you have, what condition it is in, what you have too much of, where there are gaps, and so on.

Information is different from other "hard" assets in key respects—primarily, in its *intangibility* and *reusability*.[7] It is nonetheless useful to consider those ways in which information is *similar* to other assets. In this way, many pre-existing management models, some of which are listed above, can be brought to bear on the strategic problem of knowledge productivity.

Conclusion

"The purpose of information is not knowledge. It is being able to take the right action."[8] Too often knowledge workers limit themselves to the production and distribution of knowledge, without considering how it creates value for the organization. This omission threatens the value of knowledge work—and the careers of those who perpetuate this way of thinking.

We offer the Knowledge Value Chain model in the hopes that it will spur enhancements in the productivity of knowledge processes—a key determinant of any organization's competitiveness. We do not intend it as a purely theoretical model, but rather for active deployment on the front lines of knowledge about knowledge—in diagnosing and fixing knowledge problems.

Notes

[1]That workshop is covered by a US copyright, and the term "knowledge value chain" itself is covered by a US trademark.

[2]For example, Peter Drucker: "Fifty years from now—if not much sooner—the leadership in the world economy will have moved to the countries and to the industries that have most systematically and most successfully raised knowledge-worker productivity." In *Management Challenges for the 21st Century,* Harper Business, 1999, page 158. I believe the same statement will be applicable to companies and individuals as well as countries and industries, and that the time frame will be considerably shorter than 50 years.

[3]Frederick Taylor did this for industrial work. See Andrea Gabor, *The Capitalist Philosophers,* Times Business, 2000.

[4]Michael Porter, *Competitive Advantage,* Free Press, 1985.

[5]Note that this is similar to the definition of a business process, and indeed the concepts are closely related.

[6]Michael Hiltzik, *Dealers of Lightning,* Harper Business, 1999.

[7]By intangibility, we mean that information is essentially "weightless." You can't touch or taste it. By reusability, we mean that it is not used up by being shared. For example, I can give you some information, but I continue to retain for myself.

[8]Drucker, op. cit., page 130.

Seven Key Lessons From the KVC

If I had two minutes with you in the proverbial elevator, here are the things that I'd make sure you came away with.

1. **Creating value from data requires a process.** It takes time. It has various elements that must be coordinated. It may not be immediately obvious how to do it—it takes planning and practice. The good news is that you can learn the process, and you can improve at it.
2. **Each step in the process has a benefit added—and a cost.** The skill is in keeping the former higher than the latter by minimizing the costs and barriers to value, and by maximizing the benefits. If you can do that at each step of the process, then the whole process itself will have a positive ROI.
3. **Knowledge is not power.** Knowledge and intelligence are not the end of the chain. There is a whole other set of things—decisions and actions—that need to happen before value is created. Are you fond of thinking that "Knowledge is Power"? Sorry, but it's not; the two are very different. You can integrate knowledge *with* power, in which case it becomes organizational intelligence.
4. **Great "DIKI" alone**—data, information, knowledge, and/or intelligence—**does not guarantee great results**. In business, there's no prize given for having the best information. You can, for example, have great intelligence, but then leave it unused or use it to make suboptimal decisions.
5. **Plan DOWN; produce UP; present DOWN**. The three major phases of a knowledge-based project happen in reverse order to each other. Planning happens from the "value payout" (or expected benefit) down. Production happens up through the chain. Presentation or communication focuses again primarily on the value payout.
6. **Knowledge-based disciplines**—libraries, corporate intelligence, market research, even IT—**create value for themselves only to the extent they create value for the enterprise**. There is no distinction. You need to create impact and ROI in the business functions you're serving, measured on their own terms. And you need to do this in a way that is both provable and readily communicated.
7. **There are two basic ways to create greater value**. One is "doing things right"—tactics. The other is "doing the right things"—strategy. The tactical and strategic approaches to value enhancement are complementary, and they're both essential.

References

Berkowitz, Bruce D. and Allan E. Goodman. *Best Truth*, Yale University Press, 2000.

Boyd, John. *OODA loop*, http://en.wikipedia.org/wiki/OODA_loop.

Chesbrough, Henry. *Open Innovation*, Harvard Business Review Press, 2003.

Davenport, Thomas H. *Thinking for a Living*, Harvard Business School Press, 2005.

Drucker, Peter. *The Age of Discontinuity*, Harper & Row, 1968.

———. *Management Challenges for the 21st Century*, Harper Business, 1999.

Foray, Dominique. *The Economics of Knowledge*, The MIT Press, 2004.

Haeckel, Stephan. *Adaptive Enterprise*, Harvard Business School Press, 1999.

Heuer, Richards J., Jr. *Psychology of Intelligence Analysis*, Central Intelligence Agency, 2001.

Janis, Irving. *Groupthink*, Houghton Mifflin, 1983.

Kalb, Clifford. Article in *Competitive Intelligence Magazine,* January-February 2002.

Kent, Sherman. *Strategic Intelligence for American World Policy*, Princeton University Press, 1949.

Krizan, Lisa. *Intelligence Essentials for Everyone,* Joint Military Intelligence College, 1999.

Lewis, Michael. *Moneyball*, W. W. Norton & Company, 2003.

Machlup, Fritz. *The Production and Distribution of Knowledge in the United States*, Princeton University Press, 1962.

McColl, Sir Colin. Presentation to the Business Threat Awareness Council, New York City, April 18, 2007.

Minto, Barbara. *The Pyramid Principle*, Prentice Hall, 2002.

Miller, George A. "The Magical Number Seven, Plus or Minus Two: Some Limits on our Capacity for Processing Information," *Psychology*, at http://homepage.psy.utexas.edu/homepage/class/Psy355/Gilden/MagicNumberSeven.pdf.

Pfeffer, Jeffrey and Robert I. Sutton. *The Knowing-Doing Gap*, Harvard Business School Press, 2000.

Porter, Michael. *Competitive Advantage*, Free Press, 1985.

Powell, Timothy. *Analyzing Your Competition—Third Edition*, FIND/SVP, 1993.

———. "Analysis in Business Planning and Strategy Formulation," in Ben Gilad and Jan P. Herring, *The Art and Science of Business Intelligence Analysis*, JAI Press, 1996.

———. "Researching Acquisition Candidates," in Mark N. Clemente and David S. Greenspan, *Winning at Mergers and Acquisitions*, John Wiley, 1998.

———. "The Knowledge Value Chain: How to Fix It When It Breaks," Information Today, 2001. Revised version included herein.

———. "Value-Driven Intelligence," TKA Working Paper 08-03, at http://www.knowledgeagency.com/sites/knowledgeagency.com/files/Value%20Driven%20Intelligence%20REVISED%20a.pdf

Powell, Timothy and Cynthia Allgaier. "Enhancing Sales and Marketing Effectiveness Using Competitive Intelligence," Competitive Intelligence Review, 1998.

Prescott, John. Personal correspondence.

Tversky, Amos and Daniel Kahneman. "Judgement Under Uncertainty: Heuristics and Biases," reprinted in Daniel Kahneman, *Thinking, Fast and Slow*, Farrar, Straus and Giroux, 2011.

Glossary

Here are working definitions of terms used throughout this book.

Acquire/Acquisition - KVC Transform 1; gather data according to the research plan

Action - KVC State 6; decisions that have been formulated into tactical and strategic initiatives

Action Step - a transformation needed to move from one KVC step to the next; part of a *transform* (as it is usually referred to in order to avoid confusion with KVC State 6)

Analyze/Analysis - KVC Transform 3; pull data apart and put it back together to give an insightful view of the business situation

Apply/Application - KVC Transform 5; using intelligence and decision criteria, arrive at decisions supported by the intelligence

Communicate/Communication - KVC Transform 4; transmit the analysis and backup information to a user/decision maker

Data - KVC State 1; the basic facts and figures that result from an acquisition initiative

DIKI - data, information, knowledge, intelligence

Decision - KVC State 5; a choice among competing options based on the preceding steps

Fail Point - any action step, the subpar execution of which jeopardizes the quality of the entire value chain

Feedback - KVC Transform 8 - a post-KVC step that, following implementation and value production, data are collected on an ongoing "real world" basis and fed back into the KVC

Formulate/Formulation - KVC Transform 6; plan actions to implement the decisions

Gate - test of whether the next transform or action step is worth executing

Gate Value - metric or indicator that signals whether or not the gate criterion has been met

Implement/Implementation - KVC Transform 7; execute the action plans designed to put into practice the decisions made

Information - KVC State 2; data that has been cleaned and organized

Inputs - resources invested in the knowledge or intelligence process

Input State - for any KVC step, the starting value of that step before the transformational action is applied

Intelligence - KVC State 4; knowledge that has been communicated to a user/decision maker

Knowledge - KVC State 3; information that has been analyzed

Knowledge Value Chain - a process model that describes how data, information, knowledge, and intelligence are transformed into enterprise value; also a proprietary process improvement model developed by the TW Powell Co. Inc. d/b/a The Knowledge Agency®

KVC Step - a KVC unit consisting of an input state, a transform or action step, and an output state

Outcomes - business results attributable to knowledge or intelligence

Outputs - near-term results of resource outlays

Output State - the state that results from the transformational action

Plan/Planning - KVC Step 0; the initial shared understanding with the client

Process/Processing - KVC Transform 2; organize and clean data so that is ready to be analyzed

Producer - the analyst or other knowledge professional who produces a knowledge or intelligence product

Production - KVC Transforms 1-3 collectively; also called *knowledge acquisition*

ROI - return on investment; benefits received per unit expenditures paid

SCIP - Strategic and Competitive Intelligence Professionals; formerly the Society of Competitive Intelligence Professionals

State - a stage of processing in the KVC

Transform - an action step or series of steps needed to move from one KVC stage to the next; requires expenditures of effort, resources, and time

Use - KVC Transforms 5-7 collectively; also called *knowledge application*

User - the client or decision maker who applies knowledge or intelligence to make decisions

Value - "a fair return or equivalent in goods, services, or money for something exchanged"; also State 7 of the KVC - business results or outcomes

Value Chain - a series of activities that together, in sequence, produce economic value

Value Negative - a factor that decreases the value of the transform, and, by implication, the value of the overall KVC

Value Positive - a factor that increases the value of the transform, and, by implication, the value of the overall KVC

Acknowledgements

The KVC model did not just spring from my brow one morning, fully formed. This is *Version 4*, and the KVC workshop has been given since the mid-1990s. Many people have made thoughtful inputs to the model over the years. I will thank some of these who stand out, with apologies to those whom I no doubt have missed.

Several members of The Knowledge Agency's Advisory Board played significant roles in this work. Andre Yap of the Ynnovation Groupe has consistently applied the KVC model in new ways, most recently in developing new information products and services. Patric Hale encouraged me not to write this book prematurely, and encouraged me instead to present my findings, give workshops, and test the model. I took his advice, and the whole development process has benefited from his wisdom.

Dr. Mike Koenig, former dean and now professor at the Palmer School of Information Science at Long Island University (LIU), encouraged me all along, starting with several workshops we conducted together. Mike was influential in getting me an appointment as a lecturer at LIU, where I developed the KVC model as part of a course I gave on competitive intelligence in 2004-2005.

My Master's students at LIU made astute observations about the model, and were able to apply it in their assignments. My chances to give this workshop at SCIP and other professional More recently, Guy St. Clair has enabled me to introduce the KVC to his graduate students in Columbia University's Information and Knowledge Strategy program, where it has been well-received.

My greatest reward comes when people actually use my work to help themselves. One of the best moments in "my life with the KVC" came when one former workshop paericipant told me he had quoted the KVC model in pitching for a new job—and was hired.

My teachers at the Yale School of Management had a major impact on me, my work, and my life. Art Swersey taught me operations research and production theory, much of which I have applied directly to the "knowledge economy." The late Aaron Wildavsky taught a course *Information for Decision* that was instrumental in forming my views of the role of information in the managerial decision process. Sid Winter (now at Wharton) started me thinking about how firms apply their knowledge in creating economic value. The late Ron Wippern taught me about modern portfolio theory, discounted cash flow analysis, and risk-return trade-offs—each essential in understanding the principle of *return on intelligence*.

Marya Holcombe developed her own independent seminars on corporate writing and communications, and encouraged me when the road seemed unfairly long and twisty. The late Larry Isaacson taught me that "back of the envelope" thinking—that is, informed intuition and common sense—can be a powerful business tool. Garry Brewer taught me about "the magic number seven" and other equally vivid and useful ideas.

Many people I've met through the Society of (now Strategic) Competitive Intelligence Professionals (SCIP) have been supportive along the way. Ben Gilad and Jan Herring published an early version of the KVC model in their seminal textbook *The Art and Science of Business Intelligence Analysis*. Arik Johnson pointed out the "plan your career" applications of the KVC when we were speakers together at a competitive intelligence conference in China, and has been a consistently enthusiastic supporter of the approach.

Cyndi Allgaier, with whom I've developed and given several workshops covering sales and marketing intelligence, has always been "there" for me to share ideas, enthusiasms, and frustrations. Martha Matteo, at first a good client and later a good friend, encouraged and supported this work early on. Intelligence experts John McGonagle, John Prescott, Scott Leeb, Andrew Buerschgens, and Mark Little each offered support and constructive comments. Eric Garland has been my persistent interlocutor and conscience on a range of related issues.

My consulting colleagues Howard Bleiwas and Reuben Danzing offered insightful comments and helped develop new opportunities for the KVC.

Presentation in business is key, and here I've been helped by some of the best. John Fantini has provided much of the art work. His terrific graphics realizations have helped me bring these ideas to life. Susan Murphy—who is also my "baby sister"—supplied key insights on the KVC promotion and positioning. Morgan Avery Sispoidis thoroughly proof-read this new edition, though any remaining errors are my responsibility.

My life partner Ellen Matson has had a major role in keeping me alive, well, and inspired during the long journey. She was involved in producing this book, took the time to learn what it was about, and provided significant insights on it.

Thanks to all the people that bought *Version 3.2* of the book, which we sold in hard copy from our web site. That was the first version available to an audience beyond the participants in our workshops and clinics.

Finally, but certainly not least, my warmest thanks go to the clients I've worked with over the years, both with my own firm TKA and under the banners of those great firms FIND/SVP (now ORC), PwC, and KPMG. Many of them have encouraged my work, challenged it, used it, and suggested where it needed even more work. Together they provided the economic engine that made all this possible.

T.W. POWELL

Background and Personal Statement

My Work Life

In 1996 I founded The Knowledge Agency® (TKA), a management research and consulting firm focused on competitive strategy. I am fortunate that my firm has prospered and allowed me to work with so many interesting companies and people. I have served more than 100 companies, professional and financial services firms, start-ups, and government agencies—including American Express, GE Capital, Revlon, RR Donnelley, Sony, Traveler's Group, the US Navy, and Xerox.

Prior to entering independent practice, I served as Managing Director of the Strategic Research Division of FIND/SVP (now ORC International), a global information and research network. There I founded and led a practice that executed more than 250 successful assignments in marketing and strategy for financial and information services clients.

Before that I was Business Development Manager with Coopers and Lybrand (now PricewaterhouseCoopers). There I coordinated the development and launch of several new lines of business, and developed strategies for several others. I developed and led an initiative to apply information technologies to sales and marketing processes. I co-founded the firm's competitive intelligence function and was instrumental in developing one of the earliest business knowledge systems.

I began my consulting career in the early 1980s as a "quant geek" with KPMG. I specialized in statistical modeling and quantitative forecasting, and was at that time one of the few people in the firm to be "going online." Among client projects, I led the development of a 150-sector economic model of the New York State economy that was used in evaluating revenue enhancement scenarios. I also led firmwide initiatives in new product development and strategic planning.

I previously published two books and made substantial contributions to several others. One of my books, *The High Tech Marketing Machine* (McGraw-Hill/Probus) was a Fortune Book Club selection, and is an early survey of technologies to support marketing and sales. The other, *Analyzing Your Competition—Third Edition* (FIND/SVP) has been a standard text and reference in competitive analysis.

My articles and columns have appeared in *Money, Your Company, Competitive Intelligence Magazine,* and Adweek's *Technology Marketing,* among others. You can find reprints of some of my work at www.knowledgeagency.com/content/TKA-whitepapers.

In 1999 I was elected a Fellow of the Strategic and Competitive Intelligence Professionals (SCIP), where previously, as a Director, I had co-led an initiative to develop global partners for SCIP. I founded SCIP's Sales and Marketing Intelligence (SMI) initiative, which I ran with Cyndi Allgaier, and which hosted six successful annual symposia. I was previously active in the American Marketing Association (AMA), where I served on the Services Marketing Council. After 9/11 I helped George Karshner launch the Business Threat Awareness Council (BTAC), a public-private corporate security initiative.

I love my work and it gives me great satisfaction when anyone else takes an interest in it too. I have been able to speak about it in various business professional forums worldwide. I developed and taught a graduate course, *Enterprise Intelligence,* at Long Island University and have lectured at NYU's Stern School, Rutgers, the Hartford Graduate Center, Columbia, and Yale. Those experiences have given me ample opportunity to test and refine the material in this book.

My Personal Life

I have a broad range of interests, and love learning and creating new things. Outside my consulting career, I have worked professionally as an insurance underwriter, radio broadcaster and executive, musician, psychologist, government analyst, and sound recording producer. I'm a published songwriter and a member of the American Society of Composers, Authors, and Publishers (ASCAP). I relax by playing the guitar or indulging in my other avocation, photography.

I originally planned to become a physician, and completed a biomedical engineering internship at Jefferson Medical College in Philadelphia when I was in high school. I won a full-tuition scholarship to Yale from the Cigna Corporation, a life-changing break for me.

I completed the pre-medical science program at Yale, where I gained an enduring respect for rigorous inquiry and empiricism. I then earned my BA in Psychology and Philosophy, an interdisciplinary major. My senior essay examined overall trends in psychiatric diagnosis.

By then I had had enough of school for a while, and was eager to see how things really worked. I spent several years working in the public sector on community health and education issues affecting low-income families in Connecticut and New Jersey. I then served on a financial intelligence team that helped keep New York City out of bankruptcy in the mid-1970s, while studying accounting at night at New York University's Stern School of Business. When I heard that Yale was starting a new School of Management (SOM), I returned to earn my MBA there. KPMG recruited me out of Yale, and from there you know the story.

Over time I evolved from someone who was skeptical, at times even critical, of the motives and mores of the business world—to someone who sees the economic foundation of our lives as the bedrock that keeps our "civil society" intact and thriving. Competition especially interests me because I see it as essential in building the best possible performance and efficiency in both business and public enterprise. My view of business competition was shaped by my study of evolutionary biology during my pre-med days.

Even the briefest summary of my life would be incomplete without mention of my dear family. My late parents Kay and Jim Powell were always attentive to my work, even when they professed not to understand it completely. They were both champions of creativity and of precision in both thought and language. My sister Susan Murphy has been both tireless supporter and constructive critic of my work. My life partner Ellen Matson serves as a director of TKA and also helps me immensely in every other area of my life. My beloved sons, Mike and Dave, share some of my interests—though each has achieved significant milestones and accomplishments in his own right.